Discover your True Self

The A.C.C.E.P.T.A.N.C.E. Experience

VERONICA KARARWA

Thanks v. much for your support.

V. N. Kararwa

27/05/2023

JOY OF MANY GENERATIONS

DISCOVER YOUR TRUE SELF
The A.C.C.E.P.T.A.N.C.E. Experience

Veronica Kararwa

Published by
Joy of Many Generations
+44 (0) 7914 945 246
www.joyofmanygenerations.com

Email: vero_kararwa@hotmail.co.uk

First published 2023

ISBN: 978-1-916667-02-0

Copyediting and proofreading by Dr Emem Udoh, Your Future Your Story

Cover/book design by Imaginovation Ltd.

CONTENTS

DISCLAIMER

The information and advice in this book represent the views and opinions of the author as of the date of publication. It is a resource to aid your personal growth. It is not intended to be an alternative or replacement for professional help. The book is about the author's story and personal journey from a painful, deadlocked place to a place of acceptance, personal growth, and resilience. Therefore, do not hesitate to seek professional help; indeed, I actively encourage you to seek it as required, as the contents are not intended to be a substitute for professional or medical help.

DEDICATION

This book is dedicated to my sons, Kevin Gitau Kararwa and Ian Kiriga Kararwa, for whom I wrote this. My love for them has been the driving force behind my fight to live, especially when the chips were down.

The loving memory of Kevin, whom we tragically lost to leukaemia, has been a constant source of motivation for me. His courageous fight and the challenges we faced in finding him a stem cell donor inspired the founding of the Kevin Kararwa Leukaemia Trust and served as the inspiration for this book.

FOREWORD

I have two goals in writing the foreword for this book. It is first to endorse Veronica Kararwa's lived experience as a mother managing the treatment of a terminally ill child, which led to her creation of the personal development programme as it appears in this book. My other aim is to endorse the Kevin Kararwa Leukaemia Trust (KKLT), which she launched in 2015, a year after the death of her son Kevin from Leukaemia. We at the African Caribbean Leukaemia Trust (ACLT) were proud to support this project.

When my son Daniel DeGale was diagnosed with Leukaemia in 1993, aged 6, the initial chemotherapy led to remission, but he soon relapsed. He needed a bone marrow (stem cell) transplant. We learned that as a person of African-Caribbean ethnicity, he had a 1 in 250,000 chance of finding a donor match against a 1 in 4 chance if he had been born Caucasian. There were too few donors on the register from people of his ethnicity, reducing the chances of a donor match. That was why we started the ACLT to increase the number of donors of African origin on the stem cell donor register. Our efforts yielded results in finding a match from the expanded register of donors. We were blessed with the extension of Daniel's life via stem cell donors from 12 to 21 years, for which we will always be grateful. His life would have been far longer had he not undergone the rounds of chemotherapy while awaiting the bone marrow match. It finally came, but not before the toxicity of the chemotherapy had done much damage to our son's organs.

I know from my own experience the journey Veronica has travelled. The emotions she expresses in her story could have been taken from my own lips. I met her son Kevin when he was under therapy after diagnosis, awaiting a donor match for the stem cells he needed. Unfortunately, it was not to be, and the brave young man passed away a year later.

Veronica says that the KKLT is an organisation established "in the midst of loss and heartbreak to create equal survival rates of Leukaemia for people of African and BME (Black Minority Ethnic) origin to that of those from majority ethnic groups". We at ACLT have supported the KKLT and collaborated on projects to raise and maintain awareness of the need for people of our ethnic background to join the donor registers to achieve this goal. Veronica's twin triumph is establishing the Trust and writing an excellent working programme to promote the personal development of anyone at a crossroads or dead end. This book uses the very challenges experienced as fuel for creating the best person one can be. It is accessible and brilliantly presented. We discover that the best person we can be is, and has always been, within us all, just waiting to be born.

Please use this book and its exercises. And know that while using it, your purchase will have taken us all one step further towards achieving the Trust's aim of equal chances of donor matching for BME, Africans, East Africans and other ethnic groups diagnosed with Leukaemia and other blood cancers.

Beverley DeGale OBE.
Co-Founder, ACLT
(African Caribbean Leukaemia Trust) Charity.

PREFACE

This book is a must-read for anyone at a crossroads in their life. That is when we all need a guided walk through the huge and seemingly insurmountable obstacles our perceptions throw up precisely because we are on the cusp of making enormous, life-changing decisions. At these crossroads, we feel despondent, defeated, unable to take one more step, frightened, and isolated even beyond the reach of God. You are not alone if you have felt or are feeling these emotions.

This book will hold your hand and guide you through. It is the very reason I wrote it because I, like many, have been right there at my own crossroads and know exactly how it felt. I can also tell you that but for hitting that awful junction in the road of my life, I would not be the evolved, resilient person I am today with a vision of where I should go and the tools to take me there. Now, you can join the club of the resilient and transformed.

Why did I write this book? Anyone could have written it, but I wrote it. Not because I am special in any way, it is my purpose, and you will discover your own. I am a mum of two sons, one of whom passed away from Leukaemia, triggering the dark nights of my soul and arrival at my crossroads. At that crossroads, all my education and social and professional qualifications in Mental Health and Therapy became a mass of interesting but inert theories. There is a world of difference between theory and lived experience, thought and action. Never more than at my son's diagnosis, treatment, and death did I realise the width of that gulf. And this goes to show why I had to write this book. I had an experience as an ordinary mum shared by countless others. Therefore, I had to confront the problem as an ordinary person to find solutions that ordinary people could apply. My experience led to founding Kevin Kararwa Leukaemia Trust and creating the 10-step Acceptance programme, which this book explains and which you can apply to make the right choices to become the real you, the best you, and the excellent self that you can be.

Why am I publishing the book now? Because following a series of current events, it seems the human race is moving into a new era. We are living through a time of colossal changes marked by environmental threats to the survival of our race and political conflicts that can change our systems of governance. Also, advancements in technology and artificial intelligence are having dramatic impacts on how we work and relate as human beings. We are even moving towards trans humanisation, which will blend man with machines at the biological level. At the same time, the world has undergone global turmoil with an enormous loss of life from the recent Covid-19 pandemic in 2020, with more pandemics predicted to come. These circumstances have affected world economics leading to considerable shifts in the way we work and our ability to earn secure livelihoods. It is said that 'as without so within'. Hence, all the changes 'without' make the crossroads we encounter 'within' even scarier to negotiate. Thus, more than ever before, we need an understanding of who we are and our purpose in life. When we understand life, everything we have endured takes on a new meaning as we base our lives on the real person we are meant to be.

I have set out the ACCEPTANCE programme as a step-by-step guide to discovering and becoming our authentic selves so we can make the right decisions at our crossroads. ACCEPTANCE is an acronym where the letters mean:

A – Accept Yourself

C – Core Values

C – Conduct

E – Emotions

P – Perception

T – Thoughts

A – Actions

N – New You

C – Compassion/Contribution/Connection

E- Evolve

In ten modules, I run through each core element, starting with A for Acceptance (coming to terms with the reality of who you are) and ending with E for evolving (setting in motion a cycle of perpetual growth). The book can be used on a modular basis, focusing on any of the ten elements discussed with the exercises I suggest. However, as each module builds on the one before, I highly recommend starting at the beginning and working through to the end.

The book simplifies the coaching programme that I offer either on one to one basis or as a group coaching where we dive deeper into the core elements on a modular basis for a period of 6 months.

This book will change your life. Enjoy the ride.

ACKNOWLEDGEMENTS

I want to thank my mother, Hannah Nyambura, who made sure I went to school and got an education, despite not having the good fortune to go to school herself. Mum, I wish you were here now to witness the fruits of your labour. I am forever thankful for your love, fight, and dedication to our family.

I thank my two sons, Kevin and Ian, who have always been the driving force and the source of the underlying motivation for whatever I've done. Kevin, I miss you dearly. Your illness and early death have taught me more than I can say. Your life has been a cause of my personal development to become a better human being. Ian, thank you very much for your love, support, and patience with me through our trying times. Crucially your help in ensuring your brother's legacy lives on through KKLT has been a source of strength and support for me.

Thanks to my brother Benard Ndichu who has always supported me and all my endeavours. I can never forget that time 27 years ago when you sacrificed your savings to support my travel to the UK. It was an act of love and faith in me, which remains a prime point of validating my worth and potential as a human being. I wish the whole world had brothers like you.

To my many friends, who I am unable to mention by name here, those who supported me through the holocaust of Kevin's treatment, I am humbly grateful for your prayers, practical support and words of encouragement forever engraved on my heart.

For all the Kevin Kararwa Leukaemia Trust founder members and volunteers who have relentlessly worked and supported the Trust over the years, please accept my heartfelt gratitude. Thank you very much. The Trust could not exist without you. Your work is indeed the Trust. Thank you always, and I know Kevin's spirit joins me in my applause for your dedication.

Finally, on the team, many thanks to Tet Kofi, without whom this book would not have seen the light of day. His advice and great input have been a source of strength and encouragement throughout the project. To my publisher, Pastor Joy Ani (Joy of Many Generations) and the editorial team who have shaped this book and worked tirelessly to make sure we printed on time, I am most grateful.

Now I turn to you, the readers who pick up this book, the most important supporters of all; thank you immensely for engaging with the book and, hopefully, with the Kevin Kararwa Leukaemia Trust. I earnestly pray that you find it a source of hope and strength for your life.

INTRODUCTION

"We are not given a good life or a bad life. We are given a life. It is up to us to make it good or bad."
Devika Fernando

What Is Life?

Ever wondered and asked what life is all about? During our lifetime, we experience circumstances that compel us to ask this question, and we produce answers depending on where we are, what we are doing and what is happening around us. Usually, our answers are personal and based on our individual perspectives and experience. People give answers like, 'Life is good', 'Life is difficult', 'Life is what you make it', 'Life is cruel', 'Life is not fair' and many others. However, to me, life is just life.

Life has been defined as "the aspect of existence that processes, acts, reacts, evaluates, and evolves through growth." 1 This implies that anything living must go through the above process; otherwise, it is non-living. The crucial difference between living and non-living things is that life uses energy for physical and conscious development. The process of living and growing as we know it can be challenging and painful as well as joyous and adventurous. We can then say that life is anything that grows and eventually dies. This leads us to a bigger, follow-on question. If life is about living, growing, and dying, what then is the meaning of life? What is the meaning of something that, by its very nature, is destined to die?

What Then Is The Meaning of Life?

Since time immemorial human beings have struggled with 'the meaning of life.' This question has resulted in various answers and arguments, from scientific theories to philosophical, theological, and spiritual explanations. Wikipedia gives a simple answer: "The meaning of life pertains to the significance of living or existence in general."2 However, different people and cultures ascribe various meanings to the question of life. Let us consider some brief explanations from the scientific, philosophical, theological, and spiritual perspectives.

From a scientific perspective, life is the state or quality that distinguishes living beings or organisms from non-living ones. Living things are characterised by metabolism, growth, and the ability to reproduce and respond to stimuli.

The philosophical perspective stipulates that one needs to be fully engaged with life activities that make a fuller contribution to society by investing in something larger than the needs of the individual self.

The Christian or monotheistic theological perspective states that God created man for a purpose, while the spiritual perspective talks of having a sense of connection, a higher consciousness of something universal and bigger than the individual self.

The cultural perspective of life differs between various cultures and tribes. However, many cultures believe in a higher being or beings who order our lives as individuals and communities. Within the African culture, it is generally held that an individual's life can have meaning or significance only within the community of other human beings. This cultural belief aligns with the UBUNTU philosophy – "I am what I am because of who we all are", emphasising the relationship between the individual and the community. It portrays that individuals and groups need the protective cover that community life offers if their lives will have any meaning or significance.

These perspectives of life are connected, and none of them is wrong. They just differ in their way of explanation and emphasis. It is my belief, however, that it is up to the individual to find their own meaning to life within the scope of these general explanations. As a professional and Christian, I subscribe to Paul Wong's3 psychological perspective. Wong, a Canadian Clinical Psychologist, proposes a four-component solution to the question of life's meaning as expressed by the acronym PURE. The four components are purpose, understanding, responsibility, and enjoyment.

Purpose: You need to choose a worthy purpose or a significant life goal.

Understanding: You need to understand who you are, what life demands of you, and how you can play a significant role in life.

Responsible: You and you alone are responsible for deciding what kind of life you want to live and what constitutes a significant and worthwhile life goal.

Enjoyment: You will enjoy a deep sense of significance and satisfaction only when you have exercised your responsibility for self-determination and actively pursued a worthy life goal.

From the PURE acronym, it is clear that a sense of significance permeates every dimension of meaning in our lives. However, it leaves out other vital questions about where we come from, who we are, how we should live, why we are here (our purpose) and where we are going (the end of our lives). In essence, life involves four things – Origin, Meaning, Morality and Destiny, according to Ravi Zacharias4, the greatest Christian Apologist of our time.

Most people go through life without ever pondering or actively avoiding the fundamental questions of life because it would require a deep search of their inner selves. People tend to ask these questions after experiencing a significant negative event. But how wonderful would it be if we all asked ourselves these questions without being prompted by tragic circumstances? I believe we would all have happier lives and make the world a better place. As Socrates, a Greek philosopher, said, "The unexamined life is not worth living."

Unfortunately, for most people, life 'just' happens. Some people lead a life of misery and depression, others harbour constant thoughts of suicide, others hate their lives, and some are full of anger and bitterness. We also have people destroying their lives through alcohol and drug abuse and some youths winding up in gangs. Others give up easily, becoming victims of life – hopeless and helpless, dependent and passive, leading mediocre lives of insignificance. Consequently, they die without fulfilling their dreams.

Such a life of insignificance is typically caused

by psychological dysfunctions that lead to feelings of worthlessness. It emanates from an individual's refusal or inability to deal with the normal existential anxiety and responsibility that come from confronting the realities of life – mortality, isolation, pain, meaninglessness, and freedom. As humans, we desire control over the situations and outcomes of our lives. Therefore, we become restless when we lose power or control over a situation. This restlessness leads to stress, anxiety and sometimes depression.

There are many important aspects of life that we have no control over and no power to change and must therefore live with. None of us chose to be born, nor did we choose our parents or siblings. We also had no control over our country of birth, race, gender, the colour of our eyes, and the list goes on. These attributes were given to us as gifts by our maker, and we must view them as sacred. While I fully understand and respect that people of other faiths or no faith at all will have their choices, the most important book of all time to me as a Christian is the Bible5. The Bible states that you are "fearfully and wonderfully made"5a. It also says he knew you long before you were formed in your mother's womb5b. What do these phrases mean? They mean you were made for a purpose. Please hold this thought as a fact as you continue to read.

If it is a given that there is a purpose for your life, then you might want to ask why we suffer or why there is suffering in the world. Does life have to be so hard and often so blatantly unfair?

In this book, I discuss a concept that clarifies our outlook on life and helps us come to terms with its realities. I will only attempt to look at one of many angles on how to live the life you have been given meaningfully. You have been given only one life, therefore, live it, and live it to the fullest. As complicated as life is, 'Life Is life,' 'it is what it is' as most of us have found out or rather experienced. Whether we like it or not, there are life's givens. This means that in life, 'stuff happens', or to use a Western urban slang, 'Shit happens'! How you respond or react to the realities of life shapes you and gives you meaning as an individual.

The concept that I will teach you contains ten steps that, if well followed, will help you manifest your worth and significance. It will take you on a journey of self-discovery, challenging you to go deeper into yourself to discover what you are, who you are and why you are here. However, it requires a willingness on your part to freely embark on the journey with an open mind and come to terms with some painful facts or aspects of your life experiences. It poses questions only you can answer. It also requires being honest with yourself.

The concept has helped me face life with its givens, and by doing so, I have come to find meaning in my own life. I can confidently say that, now, I have a purpose to my life, a focus that deepens my experience of fulfilment in life. The ten steps within this concept have helped me navigate life without losing focus. As I said earlier, life happens, and it is unpredictable. Armed with my concept and its ten keys, I guarantee you will be able to face anything life throws at you, find meaning and ultimately find happiness and fulfilment.

At this juncture, you might question who I am and what gives me the authority to write about life, its meaning, purpose, fulfilment, and happiness. You will understand as you journey with me in the next chapter to 2012 when I faced the darkest season of my life.

Chapter 1

FACING MY CROSSROADS

"Behind every beautiful thing, there has been some kind of pain."

Bob Dylan

IT WAS THE 20th of April 2012, a day of exceptionally warm spring weather. I remember it because it was Friday and my birthday. It started well, but after getting to work, as a therapist who normally sees clients by appointment, for some reason, I did not want to see any clients on that day. I proceeded to cancel appointments that I had for the day. At the same time, I noticed a strange physical sensation, like a feeling of dread inside my stomach. This feeling disappeared as soon as it appeared, later replaced by a sense of excitement. In preparation for my birthday, I left work early to prepare this wonderful meal for my family.

At that time, my family consisted of my two sons, a 22-year-old with his girlfriend (both at university) and a 17-year-old in college. I had been a single parent since they were both very young and my life revolved around my boys. They meant the world to me and still do and are what you could call the focal point of my life. The story was their father left when my youngest was just three months and the older one was five years old. As a mother, I had to do whatever it took to provide for and protect them. I arrived in Britain from Kenya with my two young sons on a wintry morning in 1996 at a friend's invitation. I decided to stay in the UK after my visit, and I will say that life has not been easy. However, within those years, I managed to provide for my boys by doing all sorts of jobs, from house cleaning to care work. I eventually went to university and got a Nursing Degree in pursuit of a better life for us. So, on that day, I was a proud mother of two sensible, well-adjusted, and respectful boys. I held down an excellent job in which I managed to develop myself as a qualified therapist. Really at that point in my life, things were good. I had a lot to be grateful for and no real worries to keep me awake at night.

So, on this fateful Friday, you'd have found me in my medium-sized kitchen stacked with dishes on the work surfaces. You could tell I was cooking beautiful food just from the aroma in the house. You could also tell I was as happy as a lark, singing from the heart as I fussed over my dishes on the stove. I looked at the time, and the clock read 4 pm. Just then, I heard the front door open.

My younger son, Ian, came in, his jacket hanging loosely over one shoulder and his school bag sagging the way it always did over his back. "Hi, Ian. How was it today?" I chirped at him. "Great, mum," Ian responded. "But mum, what is it with you? I could hear you singing from outside. What is the occasion?" I must have been wreathed in smiles, "Ha-ha... You know it is my birthday today," I responded. "Yes," Ian returned, "but mum, this is not your first birthday. What is so special about this one? You seem over the moon." Well, you know your brother is coming down from Portsmouth with his girlfriend," I said, trying to

3

explain myself. "Yes, but mum, this is not their first time coming down. And wow, what are you cooking? It smells nice, and who is all this food for? Are we having guests?" Ian pressed. "No," I said, "I just thought of cooking for us."

The truth is that our children know us well and our patterns of behaviour. So, they quickly determine when something doesn't follow the usual home script. "Are you sure, mum?" asked Ian. "All this food?" he continued. I tried to reassure him that our household wasn't about to be deluged by unexpected guests. "Believe me. It's just for us. Anyway, just go and change. Your brother will be here soon," I said, hugging him. Just after he left the room, the phone rang. It was Kevin, my older son. I thought he was at the station and wanted me to pick him up. I quickly grabbed the phone. "Hi, Kevin. Yes, what? Who am I with? Your brother, of course. Why?" The phone went dead. I was baffled but not perturbed. The phone rang again; I grabbed it and started speaking, assuming it was my son on the other end.

"Kevin, what is the mat... Oh, sorry, Dionne (Kevin's girlfriend), it's you. What is the matter?" The phone line went off, but not before I heard Dionne sounding as if she was crying. Now I was deeply alarmed, and my hands involuntarily started shaking. I wanted to call them back but shaking as I was, I couldn't locate the numbers on the keypad. The phone rang again (this time, it was Kevin). "Kevin, what is the matter?" I found myself asking him. "What? Doctor? What? Leukaemia?" And at that point, the phone just slid from my hands which had turned to jelly.

I had not seen my son for three weeks but had been in contact with him. During those three weeks, he'd been suffering from a cold. When the cold persisted for more than two weeks, I advised him to have his blood and symptoms checked. Kevin being an obedient son had taken the advice and he had just told me the results at that awful moment. The news was devastating.

Have you ever felt paralysed and unable to move? I sat there stupefied for a while, and although I could hear and feel my young son talking to me and shaking me, I could not respond. How could this happen? I was confused. I did not know what to feel. How would you feel? But they say the love of a mother is

5

phenomenal. In my paralysis, I had a thought that suddenly jolted me out of my stupor. "Who is with my son?" Immediately, that thought galvanised me to action, and I contacted some of my friends. The first one I called was quite far away, so she was unable to help. I then called another friend, Esther, and luckily, she did not live very far. She came running. When she arrived, she took over and quickly bundled Ian and me into the car, and shortly, we were on our way to Portsmouth. Ian, my younger son, was old enough to know the gravity of the diagnosis. He cried himself to sleep at the back of the car. After an hour and a half's drive, we arrived at Queen Elizabeth's Hospital, Portsmouth, and found they had already admitted my son. They informed us shortly after that more tests were needed to confirm the diagnosis.

That night was the most difficult night I had ever lived, a night I would not wish on anyone, a night wrought with anguish. I cannot describe the thoughts and emotions that I was experiencing. Have you ever felt like you were going crazy? Have you ever prayed in your life, like the real gut and soul-wrenching prayers? I beseeched God, all gods, and the whole universe to intervene so the diagnosis could be anything but leukaemia. I had heard about and knew what leukaemia was, but I always thought it happened *to others*. I never thought that something like this could happen to my family. But here I was, facing the most dreadful of all diseases, cancer! And it was affecting my lovely firstborn. Oh! How can I explain my feelings to you? I was a pot of sheer emotional pain and confusion. My friend helped me pray, but I would get lost in my thoughts and go silent with no words. This was like going into a stupor now and again, but she would shake me physically out of it. Somehow, I survived the night but hoped God in heaven would intervene, for the results to be wrong, different, but it was never going to be so.

The diagnosis was confirmed the following morning; my son had Acute Myeloid Leukaemia. From that moment on, we started a lengthy and painful journey. He had chemotherapy, radiotherapy, and hair loss while continuously running the gauntlet of dangerous, opportunistic infections, and the toxicity of the treatments suppressed his immune system. I experienced a roller coaster of emotions. There were bad days, good days, desperate days, hopeful times and at other times, helplessness and utter hopelessness. When I managed to sleep, I dreaded waking up in the mornings to the reality of the situation I knew I would confront. But the scariest of all was the uncertainty that pervaded the whole situation. Living with the ever-present fear of the unknown, fearing the worst yet trying to be hopeful while the situation looked dire, my thoughts projected apocalyptic visions. The inner battle of will and the fear of losing my loved one kept me suspended between reality and insanity. Sometimes, I wanted to disappear, escape it all, and quietly fade away. The pain of helplessly seeing your loved one go through pain while you cannot help them leaves you feeling useless, desperate, and hopeless. I mean, the sheer pain itself leaves you drained and paralysed.

My Son Needed A Bone Marrow Transplant

I remember this day vividly. It was a hot sunny day, and as usual, I would leave the hospital in the early morning hours to go home to my other son, sleep for a few hours and then return by midday. Kevin was doing very poorly at the time, and I particularly felt down that day. So as I was driving back, I couldn't help but notice the bright day and a big park just a few miles on my way to the Hospital.

At this time of day, the park was filled with people basking in the sun and wearing bright and colourful clothes. Seeing families sitting together and enjoying the sun made me sad because my son was fighting for his life in the hospital. My heart bled and I wished for things to be normal again. I desperately and hopelessly wanted my son to be better and for us to return to normal, but somehow, I knew this was just wishful thinking. I thought about how we take things for granted and wished I had spent sunnier days when my son was well.

When I walked into the hospital and to the ward, all I wanted was to see my son. So I headed straight into his room. On the way in, I noticed some friends sitting in the waiting area, but I was not interested in seeing or talking to them. All I wanted was to see my son. Then, in the corridor, I met one of the doctors leaving his room, and as I walked towards him, he said he wanted to talk to me and asked me to follow him.

I was scared and asked him if Kevin was okay. He said he was okay, but I should follow him, and he opened a side room. The side room was one of those clinical rooms. It had a couple of chairs, stethoscopes hanging on two pegs, an examination couch and other medical paraphernalia. He sat on one of the chairs and gestured for me to sit on the other. I opted to stand. His face was rather contorted. I was frightened he was about to dish me bad news.

At this time, my son was doing poorly. The doctor did not mince his words. With that clinical voice, he proceeded: "Miss Kararwa, I am sorry to inform you that your son has an aggressive type of leukaemia and needs a bone marrow transplant to live. We have looked in the world bone marrow registers but could not find a match." He continued to explain that bone marrow types go with ethnicity. Black matches black, white goes with white, and Asian with Asian. He explained that in the UK, we usually have shortages of bone marrow donors from black people and other minority ethnic, non-Caucasian communities. That was when I learned that Black people did not, then or now, register as donors, hence, the shortage of suitable bone marrow types for Black patients.

This news was devastating. I screamed as my legs turned to jelly, and I crumbled into a chair. The doctor could not manage my reaction, so he quickly walked out and called my friends in the waiting room. Questions were flying through my mind. *Why Kevin? Why us? What do we do? What happens next?* But what scared me the most and sapped my strength away was the thought of returning to my son's room. How was I to face him with the facts? What should I tell him? That it was over? At this point, I stopped feeling anything and felt vacant inside, as if in suspended animation. I only wanted to disappear and get away from it all. But again, the thought hammered back at me; if I disappeared, who would look after my son? Who would love him as I did? In this turmoil and with the help of my friends, I forced myself to stand up, feel my feet on the ground and bring myself back to reality.

The doctors did the job for me and informed my son. But as it goes, and in my opinion and belief, God was with us that day because we were told of a talk in the hospital about leukaemia and stem cell transplants. We both attended, and this beautiful

Afro-Caribbean lady stood up to speak. She shared how she lost her son to leukaemia due to the lack of a matching donor. After the talk, I made a beeline to speak with her. I informed her of our predicament, and she offered to help us find a donor. The lady was Beverly De-Gale, mother of Daniel De-Gayle, from the African Caribbean Leukaemia Trust (ACLT)[6]. ACLT helped us publicise my son's predicament and advertised for a major donor drive. Local and national news media reported the story, and I would say that the donor drive was a significant success. Five hundred people registered within 2 hours.

However, it was a little too late, and my son did not find a donor. Despite Kevin putting up a brave fight, he finally succumbed to the disease on 20th May 2014. He was only 24 years old.

Losing my son was a big emotional blow. You would have thought I was prepared for it, and maybe I should have been. Through the two years, I always hoped he would get better and find a donor. I never imagined losing Kevin. He was so brave and positive, and I was very proud of him. In his last days, he expressed concern about the shortage of potential stem cell donors among Black people and his desire for young Black people to know about leukaemia. He wished to start a campaign among young Black people to register as donors if he came out of the hospital. I remember his last wish was asking if 2400 people could register, i.e., 100 people for every year of his life. The African Caribbean Trust ACLT took up this task to honour Kevin's wish after he passed on.

As a grieving mother, I thought the most fitting way to leave a legacy for Kevin was to carry out his wish. I also felt it unfair that my son could not find a donor for something we were unaware of. Until Kevin's diagnosis and treatment, I did not know that stem cell donation was associated with ethnicity (Black matches Black, Caucasian to Caucasian, Asian to Asian, etc.) and that there were and still are very few potential Black donors in the registry. Therefore, I thought it necessary to found an organisation to create awareness of Leukaemia and stem cell donation to increase potential Black donors. I felt that if only Black people had been registered and in substantial numbers, my son may not have died. Kevin Kararwa Leukaemia Trust was founded on this basis. The aim is to educate and create awareness about leukaemia, stem cell registration, donation, and transplant. This will potentially increase the number of stem cell donors on the register and save lives.

You might wonder why I shared this story and its relevance to this book or the overall subject of personal development. They are as connected as bread and butter or fish and the water they swim in. My son's illness and death led me to deadlock. I was paralysed. It was like standing at a crossroads with no idea of where or how to proceed. Many events in life can leave us feeling so paralysed and deadlocked— bereavement and other transitional events like career loss, a life-changing accident, or a situation for which none of your life's experience has prepared you. I looked okay and functioning on the outside, but deep down inside, I had nothing going for me. I felt like I was full of broken glass, and if I walked or ran fast, they would cut my innards to pieces. Life for me lacked joy, meaning or purpose. I was physically and emotionally broken and dead inside.

I needed to regroup and start living and healing from within. Otherwise, I feared I would end up depressed and stuck in that quagmire forever. I had to make sense of what was happening, rise, and come to terms with my new reality.

The story is also relevant because it taught me that loss and brokenness are the most fertile soil for new growth and rebirth. In that state, I first had to come to terms with what had happened and where I was. It was a simple yet profound learning.

Lessons Learnt

During those two years of his treatment and campaign, I somehow learned and developed, despite the pain and the roller coaster of emotions. But these were lessons learned the hard way. The whole experience totally changed me as a person. It changed my worldview and made me reorder my priorities. The experience also made me ask God many questions about life and what life was all about. At the early stage of the diagnosis and start of his treatment, I underwent a deep depression. As a mental health practitioner and therapist, I never thought I could be on the other side of the diagnostic chair. I recognised the symptoms of depression but was powerless to avoid them.

Some days, I just wanted to curl up and fade away. Other times, I wanted to disappear or not wake up. There were times I did not want to move at all. I resorted to duvet diving, preferring to stay under the duvet and withdraw from the world. I realised that pain, especially emotional pain is very personal and tailored to the individual's Achilles heel, making it more devastating. No one could share this pain with me. No one could give me the certainty and assurances I desperately needed. I just wanted my son to get well and for life to become normal again. Was that too much to ask? After all, none of us had done anything so wrong as to deserve the horror of our situation. But things didn't get better.

At some point, I had to come to terms with the reality of the situation. As a therapist, I had to remember what I had taught and told my clients. Then, I had to force myself to practise those skills to cope. One of the reasons that brought me to face reality was that my son needed me. I was his world and source of strength, and if I could not cope and support him, who would? So, I had to face the reality of the situation and do whatever I needed to do despite the emotional turmoil within me. As I put those skills into action, I became stronger and was able to support my son through the journey. I can confidently say that I am now a stronger and a better person, through the entire process, from diagnosis to treatment and losing a dear son.

I learned a critical lesson during my journey, a major insight that helped me come to terms with and cope with the situation. It allowed me to move on with life, and I have also used this lesson to help my clients deal with problems and get out of depression. This 'one thing' is powerful and can be applied in all areas of our lives. And it is this one concept that I want to teach you and show you how to apply, especially when things get difficult or seem impossible. We use it all the time but are just unaware of it. Even when we know it, we do not fully appreciate its power nor use it to the maximum. This one thing is **ACCEPTANCE** and its incredible power in our lives.

Chapter 2

WHAT IS ACCEPTANCE?

"If I could define enlightenment briefly, I would say it is 'the quiet acceptance of what is'."

Wayne Dyer

THE TERM ACCEPTANCE is a noun with three different meanings. The first is the act of taking or receiving something offered. For example, if someone gives a gift and another receives it, the receiver has accepted the gift. Another definition of acceptance is about positive welcoming and belonging, favour and endorsement. For instance, a person could like someone and accept them due to their approval of that person. The third description of acceptance is that it can be an act of believing or assenting. Acceptance in human psychology is acknowledging the actual existence of a situation and recognising a process or condition, often negative or uncomfortable, without attempting to change, protest, or dispute it. This concept is close to 'acquiescence', derived from the Latin 'acquiēscere' (to find rest in) or "accepting it for what it is."

I will be expounding on the third description.

Acceptance is ceasing to fight or dispute the existence of reality. However, getting to that place of 'acceptance' is a process that requires strength from deep within. Moreover, the acceptance must be total and radical. It is "consciously choosing" unconditional acceptance. This kind of acceptance enables and empowers you to go with, rather than against, the flow of events or conditions. Have you ever tried to go against the current of a river? You would undoubtedly have experienced resistance and could not have moved as quickly as you would have liked. But what if you tried to go with the flow of the current? You will agree that you would find it far smoother to sail. The current of a river or the flow of a tide travels in only one direction at a given time, which is a reality you cannot change. If you try to go against the tide or current, you will experience resistance and need to work extra hard. The same thing occurs when you try to fight reality. You are going against the flow and will encounter resistance, manifesting as suffering and misery. However, when you accept reality, you immediately reduce the suffering that otherwise arises.

Here is another example: If you lost a loved one, you would certainly experience pain. I know that from personal experience. However, if you keep mourning your loved one by wishing they were still alive, you would be creating suffering for yourself. I am not saying losing a loved one is fair, easy or painless. Your continued wish that they were still alive, your continuous denial that they are gone, is your source of suffering and misery in addition to the pain of losing your loved one.

Pain is one of life's givens, and there is no doubt that we all experience pain at some point. Painful as it is, the idea here is to accept that your loved one is gone and will never come back. The reality is that "it is what it is", and you cannot change it. Only at this point of acceptance will you start moving on with your life. But until you reach that point, you will find that you are stuck in denial mode, anger, bitterness, guilt, depression and unable to move on. Kubler Ross talks about five stages of grief which are denial, anger, bargaining, depression and finally, acceptance[7]. We may never get over the death of someone precious, but with acceptance, we can learn to live again while keeping their memories close to us.

Acceptance helps us move on, make changes in our lives, and, more importantly, transform us from within. Acceptance is surrendering to a 'higher', more universal power and accepting things one cannot change. Acceptance is not easy. It is usually a process that requires creating a mind shift of choosing to accept. Acceptance requires some active choices from you. It does not happen by itself. It is willed. Sometimes acceptance only lasts for a short time, so you have to keep 'turning your mind' or making that mind shift over and over and over. The choice must be made every day, sometimes many times a day, hour, or minute.

The serenity prayer captures the essence of

acceptance very well, *"God grant me the serenity to accept the things I cannot change, courage to change the things I can and the wisdom to know the difference."*

In my case, for instance, painful as it was, I had to accept the reality of my son's illness every morning and many times during the day. Mornings were the grimmest times for me. I would always wake up to the painful fact that my son was in the hospital with no signs of getting better. I wished things would return to normal, but things were no longer normal. And they did not look like they were returning to normal soon. That fact alone would hit me so hard. It was too painful, but I had to face it, or I would be frozen in that mindset all day. Strangely enough, accepting reality gave me the strength and the mindset to face the day. It enabled me to support my son by being there for him. Trust me when I say this was not easy. However, in such a painful situation, I found that acceptance removed the suffering and paralysis brought on by a mindset of resistance and denial. Acceptance crucially enabled me to deal with the pain minus the suffering.

Within this concept or portal of acceptance, I have developed ten keys to unlock your potential, discover your purpose, become the most excellent version of yourself and fulfil your dreams. These ten keys will take you on a self-discovery journey, where you look within and without to become who you were meant to be — a journey to self-actualisation.

In psychology, self-actualisation is achieved when you can reach your full potential. Psychologist Abraham Maslow[8] places self-actualisation at the peak of the hierarchy of needs pyramid. This pyramid represents all the various needs that motivate human behaviour. Maslow taught that we all have a hierarchy of needs. He postulated that the lower needs for food, clothing and shelter (physical needs) are strong motivators of our behaviour until they are met. Higher needs, such as social needs and self-actualisation, are less important. The hierarchy implies that one can focus on self-actualisation only when the bottom levels are met.

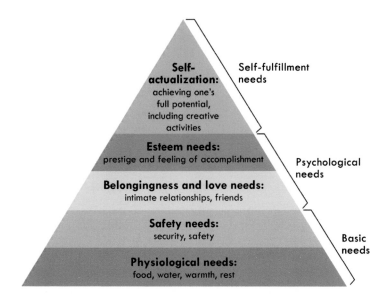

Figure 1: Maslow's hierarchy of needs.
Source: (McLeod, 2023)[9]

Characteristics of Self-Actualised People

So, what are the characteristics of self-actualised people? Here are a few, sourced from Kendra Cherry's article on Verywell mind[10].

1. They possess self-acceptance

Self-actualised people accept themselves wholly and completely, including their strengths, weaknesses, good side and flaws. They also accept others as they are.

2. They are realistic

Self-actualised people have a sense of realism. In other words, they are realistic in that they face reality as it is. They are not afraid to face the future, the unknown and the uncertainty that comes with it. They can use logic and reasoning but are at the same time able to acknowledge their fear and the uncertainty that the future holds. They are grounded.

3. They tend to be problem-centred

Self-actualised people are problem centred. They are driven by their values and take responsibility for their actions, doing what needs to be done to solve the problem. They do not play the 'blame game' or run away from problems.

4. Have peak experiences

Self-actualised people experience transcendent moments in which they are grateful for their lives and what nature offers them. They are in awe of God's creations or the wonders of the universe. They notice and appreciate the little things in life that fill them with awe, wonder, and even ecstasy.

An experience that some people call moments of profound awareness or transcendence.

5. They are independent/autonomous

Self-actualised people are quite independent and do not follow popular opinions or conform to other people's ideas. They know themselves very well and what makes them tick and fulfilled. They follow their custom-made path.

6. They are not afraid of being alone.

Self-actualised people like being alone but are not lonely. In other words, they like spending time independently to reflect, find themselves and know themselves. They are delighted in their own company. They enjoy their solitude and privacy.

7. They are spontaneous

Self-actualised people love adventure, exploration and being spontaneous. They are not confined to specific routines (though they sometimes use routines) or habitual societal norms but can try new things and follow their intuition.

Achieving Self-Actualisation

How does one become a self-actualised individual, and what does one do to become one? This is the essence of this book. This book takes you on a personal enquiry and provides you with keys to unlock the potential within you. The keys will transform, evolve and lead you to self-actualisation.

The steps to fulfilling your potential can be remembered by following the acronym ACCEPTANCE.

A – Accept Yourself

C – Core Values

C – Conduct

E – Emotions

P – Perception

T – Thoughts

A – Actions

N – New You

C – Compassion

E – Evolve

The A.C.C.E.P.T.A.N.C.E. Programme

MODULE	CHAPTER
1. Accept Yourself	Chapter 3: The First 'W' of Self-Acceptance Chapter 4: Self-Acceptance – Other Four 'W's
2. Core Values	Chapter 5: What Are Your Core Values?
3. Conduct	Chapter 6: The Value of Character
4. Emotions	Chapter 7: Master Your Emotions
5. Perceptions	Chapter 8: Perception – Expand Your Worldview
6. Thoughts	Chapter 9: Your Thoughts Are Powerful
7. Action	Chapter 10: Action For Results Chapter 11: Winning Where Others Have Failed
8. New You	Chapter 12: Happy New You!
9. Compassion	Chapter 13: Humanity's Need For Compassion
10. Evolve	Chapter 14: The Evolved Being

MODULE 1: ACCEPT YOURSELF

"Let go of who you think you are supposed to be and be who you are."

Brene Brown

Chapter 3

THE FIRST 'W' OF SELF-ACCEPTANCE

IN THE PREVIOUS chapter, we saw that self-actualised people accept themselves fully and completely, including their flaws. To assist you on your journey to self-acceptance, there are five powerful questions you need to ask yourself. I call these the 5W questions to help you explore self-acceptance, namely:

What Are You?

Who Are You?

Why Are You Here?

Where Are You?

Where Are You Going?

The first question you want to ask yourself is:

W1: What Are You?

Asking what you are may seem silly since we all know what we are. Yes, I know you know you are a HUMAN BEING. But the question is supposed to make you pause and think. It might be obvious and common knowledge that you know what you are. But do you truly know what it means to be human? Have you stopped lately and asked yourself this question deeply and more meaningfully? If you want to lead a meaningful life, your questions must start from this level, i.e., the level of a child trying to discover things and how they work. Before accepting you are human, think of what it means to be human.

Human Being

The first thing you need to accept is that you are human. I am sure you have no problem accepting this. All human beings are the same regarding their nature and needs. But we are all different in our personalities and unique expressions of self as creatures of God (as a Christian might say) or manifestations of life.

It means we come in different genders, ethnicities, races, nationalities, shapes, sizes and attributes. However, the point is we are all human beings. We are also differentiated in other ways, such as the way we are biologically wired, the way we think and act, and the way we were brought up. But one major factor is, as human beings, we are all equal in the eyes of our creator and entitled to equal rights under the natural law of the universe. In the eyes of our creator, no one is more important than the other; rather, we are all equal and worthy. You need to know that you have inherent worth as a human being. Worth that is not conveyed by state or society - a right to dignity of life.

As a human being, you have inherent rights and freedoms that are not dictated by regulations or statutes but by common sense and morals as long as no harm or loss is caused. You have rights that can never be granted or withdrawn. Thomas Jefferson put this so well in his Declaration of Independence. "We hold these truths to be self-evident, that all men are created equal, that they are endowed by their creator with certain unalienable rights that among these are life, liberty and pursuit of happiness." Thus, this is worth that nobody has the power to take away from you unless you let them. In other words, when you understand that equality is inherent and discover how it can be manifested in your life, you begin to live in the full realm of that equality. You live in it regardless of what others say and tell you about yourself. This means that you have to accept what you are, a special, valuable and unique human being with the right to be on earth just like anybody else. Do not ever let anyone, especially YOU, make you believe otherwise. Your worst enemy could be yourself. What you tell yourself about yourself and your humanity is the most important thing. They could make or break you. So please know and believe that you are not here by mistake. You are here for a reason.

This reminds me of Rosa Parks[11], an American activist in the civil rights movement best known for her pivotal role in the Montgomery bus boycott. She fought for Black people to be treated the same as Whites. She refused to give up her bus seat for a White passenger. This was when Blacks were segregated and meant to sit only at the back of public buses as second-class citizens. Her defiance in refusing to sit at the back of the bus was one of the main triggers for the civil rights movement in the United States of America. The point is that Rosa Parks knew her rights and worth. She refused to accept the low value assigned to her by other human beings, no matter how powerful they were.

Your 'manufacturer' has a 'designed' purpose for you. We all are pieces of a giant jigsaw puzzle. You are an individual and a part of a whole. We are related to one another and to the natural world. As an individual, you are unique in your own way. You have unique DNA. It is a fact that we are all different. No two persons have the same fingerprint. This fact underscores a fundamental truth that you are special and not a mistake. It means the person who designed you knew where you fit in the puzzle. Only when you tell yourself you do not fit in and move away from the jigsaw puzzle and operate as a single piece will you experience loneliness. This loneliness and emptiness will leave you lacking meaning in life. You were not created to live and operate on your own. I am persuaded that even if your only purpose is to complete the jigsaw, that alone will make you feel significant. This is because the jigsaw puzzle will be incomplete without you, and you will be incomplete without and outside of it.

Another crucial point is that the other person's worth is as much as your worth. We are all equal before the eyes of our maker. Every human being is as important as you are and deserve to be treated with respect. They have the right to be here too. We are all here for a reason and to fulfil different purposes. There are no superior purposes to the other. Take a car, for example, and all the items it needs to function. You can never say the engine is the most important part of the car; why? Because the car cannot move with only the engine. So many other items are needed for the car to work smoothly. Thus, we are all connected and need each other. No other human being is more important or special than the other. It is just through human constructs that we classify other human beings as more important, superior, special, or worthy than others.

As a human being, you probably fall under several categories. It is advisable to classify yourself in one or two of these categories to accept yourself fully.

These are: -

1. Gender

What gender are you? Male or female? This might seem obvious to most of us, but as a mental health professional, I know better than to assume that this is obvious. Today, many people struggle with accepting the gender they were born with. In my line of work, I have seen that most of these people suffer from mental health issues. The confusion emanates from the conflict between reality and what they feel, think and believe they are or should be. It bleeds another issue of getting the family and society to accept what they believe they are. It is a huge psychological problem for some people who become depressed and unhappy. Many end up feeling confused and disturbed, indulging in reckless behaviours, like taking drugs which ruin their lives. My emphasis is that you must first accept your biological reality.

I understand that gender dysphoria is more complicated than this explanation, and I know the feelings are real and painful, but the reality is what it is. First, come to terms with and accept reality as it is. The second level of acceptance is accepting feelings and the conflict within the self. This process brings calm and ushers in deciding what to do and how to live. However, when one is stuck in denial and wishes things were different while reality stares you in the face, it brings inner emotional turmoil that results in depression, reckless behaviour, and misery

Besides gender dysphoria, there is also the issue of the respective roles that each gender plays. In the natural world, the biological makeup of each gender is different. Both males and females are human beings, created equal but different in design. The difference is what makes each of them unique. Different does not mean inferior or superior. It means they were made for different purposes. Purpose denotes the original intent of the creator. The purpose of something determines its nature, design and features. When we do not understand and appreciate our God-given differences and purposes, we become confused and do all sorts of things.

Women, as well as men, are likely to have

conflicts if they do not understand why they are made as they are. We have different roles to play based on our genders, but the roles have reversed in our current society due to economic demands. Confusion about gender roles, responsibilities and purpose leads to breakups in relationships, marriages and families. We now have single-parent homes and same-gender families, not to mention dysfunctional families. As a result, our society is broken. In life and practice, the two genders are supposed to complement each other, work in harmony and produce something beautiful.

Another vital aspect we must address is our treatment of the opposite sex, especially how males treat the female gender. For ages, males have dominated females, leading to domestic violence and discrimination against females in virtually all spheres of life, social, political and economic. It is an old truism that if you do not know how something functions, you will likely misuse or abuse it. This happens when we do not understand the inherent nature and worth of a woman or a man. If we do not know what they are, how can we fathom how they should function together as human beings?

These thoughts lead us to several pertinent questions that you must answer.

Are you female or male?

Do you appreciate how you are designed to function?

Do you know your purpose and inherent worth?

Do you know the value you bring to the human race?

What role are you playing, and what are your responsibilities?

How do you view and treat yourself and the opposite gender?

Accepting our humanity and the uniqueness of each human being is essential for developing a healthy society.

2. Race

This is another area that requires acceptance. While most people accept their race comfortably, some are not comfortable in their own skin. They would rather be of another race of their choice. There are different reasons why someone would prefer another race to theirs. When this preference causes you distress, you have a major problem that affects how you see yourself and others. This could lead to unhappiness. It may seem easy to change your behaviour by copying your preferred race, bleaching or toning your skin excessively, shunning your race, and pretending to be of the other race, thus, becoming unauthentic. You become somebody you are not.

In most cases, you neither fit in with the preferred race nor your race. Consequently, you lose your sense of belonging, which can cause psychological problems and lead to depression. In Maslow's hierarchy of needs, which I refer to many times in this book, one of the stages of actualising is having a sense of belonging. When one lacks a sense of belonging from within and without, it causes distress and unhappiness. And it becomes challenging to self-actualise and feel fulfilled in life. At the beginning of this chapter, I stated that human beings are the same in nature and their needs. A sense of belonging is one of the essential human needs to lead a fulfilling life.

There is also the psychological or mental attitude towards your race, where you feel inferior and inadequate compared to another race. This mental attitude will cause low self-esteem and a lack of confidence in your abilities. As a result, you would end up selling yourself short of your true potential. Historically, Black people have been discriminated against by Whites since the era of the slave trade and colonisation. The various acts of dehumanisation of the Blacks (taking their identities, killing and maiming them, making them believe they are less human and not worthy in many ways) have made most Black people believe today that they are unworthy or incapable, unlike the so-called superior race. But that is not true.

There is no superior race. We are all human beings with different shades of colour on the outside. We all have different capabilities; all we need is to believe in ourselves, employ the right attitude, be in the right environment and have the right tools. As a human being, I have learned that it is

44

up to you to decide what you are and what you are worth to others. Remember that all human beings are equal, and each person has an intrinsic value. No one has the right to violate the rights of another. This fact alone should start building your confidence in what you are. My attitude and thoughts about myself positively changed when I internalised this fact.

Let me remind you that it is wrong to discriminate against others because they are different or not members of your tribe, race or ethnic group. Please accept that even you, yourself, did not choose your race. You had no say in where you were born and the family you were born into, just like the other person you discriminate against. Please remember that nothing makes your race, ethnic group or tribe superior to another. Therefore, understand and accept that we all belong to one human race, irrespective of our ethnicity.

3. Physical Attributes

Another source of issues is people not liking and accepting the physical attributes they were born with. Some people live miserable lives because they are shorter than others, taller than others, not as handsome or beautiful as others, and don't have a particular eye colour, hair texture or nose shape. Some people born with disabilities spend most of their lives complaining, hating themselves and being angry with others. They focus on what they do not have or would like to have. They fail to appreciate life and what it can offer. Again, in these cases, radical acceptance is required. Accepting what is and learning to live with what you were endowed with makes your life bearable and enjoyable. As I said at the beginning, life is unfair, and some people are dealt a bad hand. If that is you, what would you like to do, complain your whole life and live miserably?

Surrendering to what is brings relief and solutions and makes you focus on what you can do and bring to the world. Many people were born disabled; they accepted themselves and found themselves impacting their world. This is because acceptance brings change. My focus here is accepting things you cannot change. If there is something you can do to change your situation or disability, by all means, do so. But for what you cannot change, acceptance is the key, which must come from within. Remember, none of us chose to be born; neither did we choose where we were born, our parents, the colour of our skin, physical features and so on. If we all had a chance, we would have given our maker specifications for our size, height, complexion or other physical attributes. Sadly, we did not get that choice and had to make do with what we were given.

To crown this chapter, I want to talk about one person who really inspires me, Nicholas James Vujicic[12]. Nicholas was born without both arms and legs, but this has not stopped him from becoming, in my opinion, who he was meant to be. His parents did not know what to do when they gave birth to him. He struggled in his childhood to come to terms with his condition. He even experienced bullying at school and suffered depression, as would anyone in his situation. However, Nicholas finally accepted himself fully regarding how he was made and bingo! He is now a renowned public speaker. He inspires others to overcome obstacles in life. Nicholas does most things you and I can do. Actually, he does most things better than most people with both arms and legs. Why? Because he did not let his physical attributes hinder him from becoming who he was born to be. I bet you he struggled at an early age, seeing he was so different to others. Yet when he accepted himself fully, he was able to do and become who he is today. That is the power of acceptance. I urge you to look him up and read his story and that of many others who have overcome such obstacles.

Do not let what you were endowed with or what you do not have become a barrier and stop you from living a fulfilled life. Early on in this chapter, I talked about how everyone has intrinsic worth and a purpose to fulfil in this world. Nicholas could have written himself off due to his physical attributes. People and society might also have written him off, but God or divine intelligence knew his purpose, who Nicholas really is and how he functions. Nicholas now inspires and transforms lives. He is simply fulfilling his true purpose in this life.

Please note that I am not saying it is easy. Of course, it is not! Coming to terms with your deficiencies is not easy. However, once you come to terms with what 'is' and accept it fully, inner change occurs. You can focus on your strengths and abilities like Nicholas.

Chapter 4

SELF-ACCEPTANCE – OTHER FOUR 'W's

W E CONTINUE OUR discussion on the 5Ws of self-acceptance. This chapter focuses on the following questions:

Who Are You?

Why Are You Here?

Where Are You?

Where Are You Going?

W2: Who Are You?

Who are you? This question is usually tough and personal. Have you ever asked yourself who you truly are? Now that you have accepted what you are, your gender, race, and physical attributes, how do you define yourself as an individual? In a sea of billions of humans, who are you? What makes you, you? What makes you unique from others?

As stated earlier, humans are the same in nature and their needs, but each is unique in their personality. So, is it your name, associations, role and function in society that makes you unique? It is not! The question of who we are is complex because we mean different things to different people. For instance, you are a son to your mother, husband to your wife, father to your children, brother to your siblings, an employee of a company, friend to your friends, neighbour to your neighbours, CEO of a company and so on. Yet, that is not the focus of this discussion. The question is: who are you? Most people pass through life without asking themselves this pertinent question. This is because our culture and society dictate who we should be, what we should look like, how we should behave, the titles we should have and other attributes.

We go through life without taking the time to ask ourselves who we truly are. We simply follow the instructions imposed by our society. Sometimes, we are so busy conforming to our cultural norms, seeking acceptance at the expense of whom we could become. We relegate our authentic genuine self to the background so our 'fake self,' our assumed identity, can be seen. We copy others and go with what is popular even when we know it is not who we are. We choose a borrowed life and spend our lives not knowing our true selves, what we are capable of, or why we are here.

As a Christian, I can say this: God does not work through fake or plastic people. He looks for a genuine, original person to work with. It is through authentic people he can impact the world. It is also true that you cannot express who you are when you are busy trying to be someone else or trying to ingratiate yourself with others. You must accept yourself and stop worrying about what others will say about you.

Wayne Dyer[13], the father of motivation, explains that we are all spirits in a body and that who we are is an invisible being. He states, "you are a spirit being having a bodily experience, not a body having a spiritual experience." This spirit being is not touchable and does not occupy space. Deepak Chopra[14] describes this as our conscious being, and Myles Munroe[15] also talked about who you are as a spirit being. The Bible says that we were created in God's image. As taught in Christianity, God is invisible, infinite, untouchable, immortal and omnipresent. Myles Munroe says that our image of God is that of the above qualities, not the body. Basically, we are a spirit. Your spirit is the part of you that is not physical. It is that part that consists of your character and feelings, in other words, your soul. Your spirit is indestructible; it wants to grow, create and expand to new horizons.

However, our egos take over and rule our lives, and we forget who we are and our capabilities. In the Bible, God gave man dominion on earth, to rule over all other creations and to be creative[16]. This personal journey that you will be taking will introduce you to your authentic self, and you will realise how much power and potential you have within you as a spirit being. But first, you must accept that you are a child of the most-high God, created in his own image and with great capabilities[17]. If you believe and internalise this, you can achieve anything. Once you know who you are, you grow in strength, resilience, and confidence.

I hope so far, a picture or idea is emerging in you.

If you have an idea of who you are or know who you truly are, how confident are you in being you? Can you be yourself without succumbing to the influence of others? And are you truly living your life? Are you authentic? If not, what is stopping you?

W3: Why Are You Here?

Have you ever wondered or asked this big question: Why am I here? In the previous chapter, I mentioned the four main questions of meaning, purpose, morality, and destiny. This question focuses on purpose. In other words, what is your purpose? Why are you here on this planet and at this point in time? This is a crucial question that we need to ask ourselves. Most people go through life without knowing or discovering why they are here and what they were meant to do. This ignorance leads to a purposeless life, misery, regrets and depression. As mentioned earlier, no human being was born by mistake, even if your birth was unplanned by your parents or was caused by rape. Your creator knows you, and he brought you forth for a purpose. Hence, our difference and having different areas of reward or what I call 'gifting.' These life events and circumstances - where we were born, our environments and experiences - shape our thinking and behaviours, and we end up lacking self-worth.

Sometimes, it is not even life experiences; it is just that we never get around to asking ourselves this question. We are so busy following the script written for us, playing by the rules of society, earning a living, and essentially leading a mediocre life. We never pause to ask what we are here for and what we are meant to do. We are all meant to make a difference in our world in diverse ways tailored to our uniqueness. The question is, how are you impacting your world? What legacy will you leave after spending time in this world? Most people are obsessed with accumulating material wealth, gaining fame, and becoming popular. While these things are not bad in themselves, if they are the sole focus of your life, your existence becomes shallow, self-centred, and utterly forgettable. Your *why* should have a legacy written all over it. Find your area of gifting, and therein lies your legacy. But even then, you still must choose to live a purposeful life. Remember, we are all connected to each other, nature, and to God.

For this reason, your given talents and purpose are not meant for you alone. They are intended for others and God. It is how you connect with your world, the part you play in the huge jigsaw puzzle of life. As Myles Munroe stated, "An apple tree does not eat its apples," and it is the same for human beings. Our purpose is to serve others, our planet and God.

W4: Where Are You?

Now that you have pondered who you are and why you are here, the next question might alarm you: where are you? You might wonder why you need to know where you are. Every time we start a journey, we must have a starting point and an endpoint. This question pertains to the last of the four elements of life that we discussed at the beginning, which is Destiny. Every beginning has an end. The question is, where are you with your destiny? Do you know where you are going or your endpoint? Once you know where you are going, the starting point becomes relevant and essential. Before you embark on any journey, you need to know where you are going, and then you can plan how to get there and how you will make the journey. If, for example, you are driving to a certain destination and say you are using a Sat Nav, when you key in your destination, the Sat Nav must first locate where you are and, from there, plan the route to your destination. The same applies to our life journey. We must start and accept where we are when we embark on growth and self-discovery.

Hence, the third W asks the question, 'Where are you?' Where is your location in relation to where you want to go? In other words, where are you in key areas of your life, or what have you managed to achieve concerning who you want to become? Or have you already arrived? That is also a possibility, though an unlikely one. And the other question is, do you even have a destination in mind? If you do, what does it look like? What do you envision for your future? Do you have a vision and a plan for how to get there? If not, why not? The Bible says, "my people perish for lack of vision"[18]. It is also true that life without a vision is purposeless.

To answer the question of where you are, look at areas of your life that need improvement. For a fulfilled life, you want to approach this question holistically. If you develop one area of your life and leave the other, you will have an unbalanced life. Or you could be excelling in some areas of your life while the other aspects look like they have been in a car crash. The idea here is to evaluate different areas of your life, identify areas that need developing, and take a compass reading on where you are and where you want to go. The following are the key areas you should consider:

Physical Health

Do you keep yourself healthy? What are your eating, drinking, smoking, exercise, and sleeping patterns? If you are on medication, are you taking them as prescribed and doing what you can to keep yourself healthy? Remember that if you do not look after your physical health, achieving what you want in life will be difficult. Your body is the only vehicle that will get you to your destination. If you fail to fuel, maintain, service and do regular MOTs on your 'vehicle', it might suffer a breakdown before you reach your destination. It is, therefore, paramount that you assess where you are in terms of your physical health. It would be best to start doing all you can to become and stay fit for the journey. Healthy eating, regular exercise, the cessation of unhealthy habits like excessive smoking and drinking, getting enough sleep and meditation all form part of a good health regimen.

Mental/Emotional Health

Are you keeping yourself mentally and emotionally well? There is a saying that there is no well-being without mental health. We are all prone to getting mental health breakdowns if we are not careful and aware of what creates and constitutes good mental health. Any stressful life event can cause a mental health breakdown. Home and work-life stress can cause mental health problems. There are so many life issues that can cause mental health problems. How do you manage everyday stress? Do you know your stress limits? Do you know when to ask for help?

To most people, admission of mental health problems is shameful, representing a failure in life. So many suffer mental health problems in silence. They are afraid to admit they are struggling in specific areas of their life. They undergo emotional pain and turmoil before a full mental health breakdown. Others suffer miserably and fail to enjoy life as they should. Many reasons and elements of life can cause mental health problems, and we will be looking at some of these reasons later in the book. For now, let me ask you, where are you regarding your mental health? What do you do to keep yourself mentally well? How do you deal with stress? Which habits do you indulge yourself in that can ruin your mental wellness? Here are some major habits that can cause chronic mental health issues, drug and substance abuse, including smoking and excessive drinking, toxic relationships, and lack of purpose in life. They say that an idle mind is the workshop of the devil. When one lacks purpose, they indulge in harmful habits as they do not know who they are and where they are going. Otherwise, when you know where you are going, then you know which roads to avoid. This question is for you to assess yourself and see where you are in terms of your mental health so you can start paying attention and making changes. To help your mental health, know the limits of what you can manage and what you cannot handle. Seek help early enough when stressed. Take time off to unwind, avoid harmful habits, and choose great friends. You need a supportive network of family and friends, and meditation would help a great deal.

Spiritual Health

How is your spiritual health? Are you anchored to your source? Remember the first question about your origin; where did we come from? Our strength is from our source. Where will you be anchored when things go wrong and the storms come (which will surely happen)? If you are not anchored to your maker, you will be blown away by the storms, no matter how well you think you are doing. Your foundation should be anchored on this one force, the power and gravity of your maker. Most people believe in a larger, bigger, and more powerful being than themselves. Christians call that being God; Muslims, Allah, and others call it the universe or divine forces.

We all came from somewhere. We did not pop out of thin air. Like small children, we run to our parents for protection and support when we are threatened or insecure. The big problem nowadays is that most people do not believe in a higher being. They believe in themselves or their egos. Little wonder when challenges beyond their capacity occur, they have nowhere to go or anyone to turn to. It is understandable in a science and material-based world when they say that they cannot believe in something that is invisible, and so in their mind, such a creator does not exist.

However, God's existence surrounds us. Your existence is one of the key pieces of evidence. As indicated earlier in the first chapter of this book, you are wonderfully and fearfully made, and that you do not know how you were made might be understood as a reason to believe there is a maker or designer who designed you. And that is the person we go to when things become unbearable and beyond our capabilities. Our creator, God, is our source, keeper, sustainer, provider, and everything. When we remain anchored to him, he gives us strength, hope and a reason to live. Learn to surrender to this force, especially when pain and situations become unbearable and beyond your control.

Social Health

How are you connected with others? In other words, how is your relationship with the significant people in your life? How do you maintain relationships with them? No one is an island. We need one another and must sustain our relationships. Sustain love relationships, business relationships, friends, family, colleagues, neighbours, and everybody who engages with us.

Furthermore, we all need each other. In Maslow's hierarchy of needs, he mentions that all humans need to feel they belong. This builds our self-worth and significance. Our social connections give us a sense of belonging and help us complete our sense of identity. Consequently, we all need others as well as to be needed by them.

Financial Health

The Bible says that money solves all problems[19]. If this area of your life is suffering, there is no doubt that your life is out of balance. Nowadays, we need money to navigate most areas of our lives, and although money is not everything, it is vital for a meaningful life. Are you managing your financial affairs well, or are you in debt? Are you struggling to keep up with the essential payments? What is the overall state of your financial health?

Acceptance of your holistic being is crucial for your well-being. Taking stock of where you are in all the essential components of life is paramount for a fulfilled life. Your physical, spiritual, financial, and social well-being are all important. If one element is out of balance, it will contribute to your unhappiness. You cannot always have complete balance in all areas of your life. However, you can achieve balance by being aware of them and working towards them. Looking critically at each component and assessing it in terms of where you are and where you would like to be will give you a clear map for your journey towards becoming what you were meant to be.

But here is the thing, when some people take stock of where they are and where they would want to be, they get discouraged, hate themselves, blame others for their failures, give up on themselves and lose hope of ever becoming or achieving their dreams. The idea of taking stock of where you are in your life is not to make you feel sorry for yourself or encourage self-loathing. The aim is to help you achieve acceptance of your reality, whatever it may be. Then you can take responsibility for why you are where you are without judgement or self-recrimination.

The aim is to motivate you to chart a new course and move towards your goal or vision. It is Wayne Dyer who clearly states that you are fully responsible for where you are at this point in your life by the decisions and choices that you have made earlier in your life. So, do away with the blame game, including blaming yourself, your parents, the government, and your relatives. Instead, accept the reality of where you are. Then, decide what changes to make in each area of your life to align yourself with your vision. If you do not have a vision or goal in life, then it is high time you sat down and set up your goals and a vision for your life.

I found out what the power of acceptance meant when the penny dropped for me. I had to accept where I was and its reality and had to make that crucial decision of either remaining in the same place or moving towards a better place. But to move to a better place, I needed to change many areas of my life. The realisation was painful and difficult, but I knew I had no choice if I wanted to be in a better place than I was." After all, they say, "no pain, no gain."

Jim Rohn[20], one of the best motivational speakers, said, "For things to change, you have to change, and for things to be better, you have to become better." For example, if you are overweight and need to lose weight for whatever reason, you must first accept that you are overweight. Then you decide on your ideal weight and plan for what, where and how to lose weight. Of course, this is not a one-off decision or action, not at all, but it is the starting point. Without acceptance that you are overweight, there will be no decision or plan to lose weight. What follows is the action plan required to reach the goal: calorific intake, change of diet, change of habits, exercise regime and so on. The plan needs to be detailed with a commitment to its implementation. However, I have seen people aware of their weight problems but unwilling to accept and change their eating and other bad habits. They would instead choose to hate themselves and blame their weight on everything but their own lifestyle habits.

W5: Where Are You Going?

Every journey has a beginning and an end. We all know that we must pass away at some stage, and if you are alive, you know that you will die. What matters is what happens in between. The big question is, how will you map your journey? What do you want to do, and in which direction will you travel? What do you want to achieve or do while here on this planet? What kind of footprints do you want to leave? What kind of choices are you making for your life?

Whither lies your destiny? What are your goals in life? It is said that "if you don't know where you are going, any road leads there." Do you know where you are going? Do you know what you want to achieve in life? Do you have a dream or a vision? The Bible says that without a vision, people perish[17]. Without goals in life, you become a failure.

It is also said that "if you know where you are going, then you surely know which roads and directions not to take." This means that when you know where you are going and what you want to achieve, you will be careful not to indulge in behaviours that sabotage your journey. You know which behaviours, habits, and attitudes to adopt as they concord with your goals and destination. A pianist or surgeon must take diligent care of their hands. A pilot cannot afford to have an alcohol problem. An athlete must retain peak fitness. When you know where you are going, your habits, attitudes and behaviours should align with your goals. These choices include your choice of friends, the places you go, the pastimes you indulge in, the books you read, the shows you watch, and the list is endless. Lead a disciplined life - there are things you would not do because they are not aligned with your destiny.

Do you know where you are going? Do you have goals? Do you have a plan for your life, or are you just living or existing? If you do not have a plan for your life, this is the time to pull one together. Another old saying says: "failing to plan is planning to fail." Therefore, what are your plans for your future? Accept where you are and map your journey towards your destination. Make a blueprint for your life.

On this journey, it is best to ask if your goals are aligned with your purpose and who you are. Are my goals driven by what others expect of me, and what is popular?" As a mental health practitioner, I have witnessed and counselled many people who lead miserable lives of depression and other mental health problems emanating from choosing the wrong careers. These careers were directed by their parents or influenced by others. They never stopped to ask themselves, "Who am I?" "What do I want?" "What am I good at?" Who do I want to become?

I once counselled a medical practitioner who was a surgeon. He was referred to me after a couple of failed suicide attempts, of which the second was nearly successful, but he survived. During our sessions, it transpired that he excelled in school to please his parents, especially his father, who never appreciated him and his success despite his hard work. Deep down, he always wanted to act. He said when he was doing drama, he felt complete and in his element. However, his parents shunned drama and what it entailed. So in favour of his parents, he pursued medicine. This career came with prestige for the family but to the detriment of his well-being. Hence, his depression and suicide attempts. He found life not worth living despite having a great and prestigious career. Deep down, he was unhappy and doing something he did not enjoy. As a result, he got himself in a lot of trouble at work and risked being struck off. However, when we explored his source of unhappiness, he slowly understood the problem and what he needed to do. The changes and the journey he had to make required acceptance and a lot of courage. But he reported feeling alive and hopeful once he decided. He realised he was losing his happiness as a result of living to please his parents.

Meanwhile, the parents were not aware of the inner conflicts that tortured him, and his father did not even appreciate the sacrifice the son was making to bring praise to the family name. The realisation that it was not about his parents or society but finding himself, who he was, what he wanted and who he wanted to become liberated him and gave him a purpose and reason to live. While still working as a surgeon, he enrolled himself in drama and acting classes and reported great satisfaction and enthusiasm for his future.

The story above demonstrates the power of acceptance. Again, it shows that once you are able and ready to accept what the problem is and come to terms with reality, no matter how difficult and painful it is, then and only then can change occur. But this only happens when we are ready to go on a self-discovery journey, which is tough but worthwhile. Self-discovery requires the willingness to face and confront difficult emotions and barriers within. Most of these barriers have developed as cultural beliefs embedded in how we have been socialised and brought up, our experiences and the environment we grew up in. Although the process of confronting, identifying, and releasing ourselves from them can be challenging, it is worth the while.

MODULE 2: CORE VALUES

A highly developed values system is like a compass. It serves as a guide to point you in the right direction when you are lost."

Idowu Koyenikan

Chapter 5

WHAT ARE YOUR CORE VALUES?

FIRST, LET'S LOOK at the word value. One dictionary definition of value is "the regard that something is held to deserve, and the importance, worth or usefulness of something." A second dictionary definition is, "Principles or standards of behaviour, one's judgement of what is important in life." This chapter will focus on the second definition.

Let me ask you, what are your living standards and what is important in your life? What defines you as a person, and what are your boundaries or the things you would never do? Usually, people derive their value system from their family, society and culture. Cultural values are typically based on the culture's determination of what is good and important. Simply put, values are based on moral systems and lasting beliefs or ideals shared by society about what is good or bad, right or wrong, desirable or undesirable. In other words, these values become one's principles of conduct and largely guide our behaviours. As indicated earlier in the first module, we are all different in many ways. Our differences include our upbringing, personal experiences, and value systems. As a result, we all have different moral and belief systems shaping our behaviour. As an individual, you have carved out the value system that governs you and your behaviour based on your culture and the beliefs arising from it. The personal ethics and ideals that guide your when making decisions, building relationships and solving problems are your core values.

Now let me ask, what are your core values? What values govern your behaviour? What are your moral values based on? Have you consciously identified the personal core values that govern your behaviour? Do you have personal core values that guide your decisions in daily life? Identifying the core values that are meaningful in your life can help you to develop and achieve personal and professional goals. By knowing what these values are, you can find the jobs, companies and relationships that align with your ideals. Knowing your core values enables you to make other important life choices that tell you how to behave in challenging situations.

Most of us need to know clearly what our core values are. We need to understand what is most important to us instead of focusing on what our society, culture, and the media tell us to do, even when it may be wrong for us. Without undergoing a discovery process, it is challenging to identify your personal core values. You may speculate and idealise what you should value, but knowing and accepting what you value takes effort. Personal core values are an essential part of who we are. They highlight what we stand for. They represent and project our unique, individual essence and provide us with a personal code of conduct.

When we honour our core values consistently, we experience fulfilment. However, we become incongruent and more likely to slide or escape into bad habits when we don't. Lacking clear core values makes it easier to regress into childish, unconstructive behaviour to uplift ourselves. Our mental, emotional, and physical states suffer when we do not honour our values.

Core values do not magically appear by themselves. Instead, we establish them by discovery and wilful thought. Moreover, our core values change and evolve throughout our lives as we grow and change.

Examples of Core Values

There are many more core values you might want to adopt. You can find them in an internet search for "core values". It is useful as it may help expand the possibilities you might like to consider. People who live their values experience a sense of fulfilment and stability. Find some examples of core values below.

Honesty

Honesty is telling the truth and living the truth and doing as one says and saying as one does. It is being straightforward and trustworthy in all your interactions, relationships, and thoughts. Being honest requires self-honesty and authenticity.

Humility

Humility is being humble, without haughty pride and living a life of gratitude and appreciation for what you have. A humble person is always growing because they are ever ready to learn from anybody. They are not boastful or constantly proclaiming their achievements.

Integrity

Integrity means showing good character. It is behaving in a way that manifests the simple but colossally important virtues that enable diverse people to live together as a community. Integrity includes virtues like doing what is right even when no one is watching, keeping your word and promises, and being reliable and trustworthy.

Generosity

Generosity is giving willingly from the heart without expecting anything in return. It could be the giving of your time, money, emotions and other material and spiritual resources you possess.

Independence

Independence is the ability to stand in your truth without being coerced. It is being confident to stand alone, even when others go the other way.

Responsibility

Responsibility is taking ownership of your actions, good or bad, and being accountable for the choices you have made. Taking responsibility is not blaming others or being inappropriately defensive when challenged.

How To Discover Your Core Values?

Values are not selected; they are rather discovered and revealed through a process of self-questioning and answering. When you start this process, ensure you are in a calm state of mind and peaceful environment. Then start by asking yourself what values you honour when you are happy. Next, flip this round and ask yourself, what value is being suppressed, undermined or violated when you are very angry?

I would advise working with a coach, as they can provide helpful prompts and direction, but you can also do it yourself. When working by yourself, it is important to apply self-honesty, patience, and determination.

The following questions can also help to start you off.

What values are essential to your life?

What values represent your primary way of being or who you really are?

What values are essential to supporting your inner self?

Core Values Exemplified

I once coached a woman who had lost her job after disagreeing with her boss. She was a very ambitious lady who had worked very hard in her career and became head of a financial department in a prestigious organisation. She noticed some discrepancies in the financial figures and raised queries about them. Instead of the CEO answering her questions, he invited her for lunch and during lunch, he indirectly offered her a higher position if she dropped the matter. However, he also subtly threatened consequences if she decided not to drop the matter and accept his offer.

Back home, she contemplated the content of the meeting and felt something was not sitting right with her. She had asked for a fortnight to respond. During those two weeks, she was filled with dread and could not cope with her workload or concentrate. She told me that in those two weeks, she felt like she was going crazy. On the one hand, she had a chance to advance her career and earn more money; on the other, she feared losing her job if she pursued the matter. She had worked so hard to develop herself and get into that position. She was locked in the horns of this dilemma. At the end of the two weeks, she could no longer stand the inner conflict, so she confronted the boss and resigned.

When she came to me, she was an emotional wreck. She was clearly undergoing depression. Through coaching, we looked at what caused the conflict within her and why she resigned instead of taking the offer on the table, which looked more attractive. She said she could not do it because everything about the offer went against her faith. We unravelled her faith, and we came down to her moral values. She could not violate her moral values, which included honesty, reliability, responsibility, accountability and loyalty. At the time, she did not know nor could she articulate her core values and their role in her life and decisions. She discovered who she really was through the self-discovery process precipitated by her experience. She realised the cause of the conflict was the fight between violating her values and taking the juicy offer. Ultimately, she automatically went with the core values that lay unarticulated but very present in her psyche. Once she realised this was what happened, the conflict within her evaporated.

She started feeling alive and proud of the decisions she had made. She knew it was the right decision and felt confident in herself and her prospects of finding another job. Two months later, she had another job in a bigger role with better pay.

To top up the above story, I find the tale of Joseph[21] in the Bible an excellent illustration of how we use personal core values. His master, Potiphar's wife, approached Joseph to sleep with her. However, Joseph, a God-fearing man with a strong moral code of conduct, refused her advances and was falsely imprisoned.

These days, very few people would refuse such a proposition, as attested to by many high-profile scandals published in the media. On the contrary, many would view it as an honour and a chance to advance their careers by being linked to Royalty. They would even kiss and tell and might profit from their exploits via media publicity as celebrity scandal sells. Such is the culture we are in today. But this was not the case with Joseph.

Of course, by divine providence, Joseph later rose in his own right to become the nation's Premier. His decision to refuse her wooing was guided by several core values, integrity, respect for himself and his master, and self-control. Most people cannot boast of these core values, but they are very important and helpful for leaders or those who aspire to high office. Even in the home and society, such values help to cement and protect family and community life.

MODULE 3: CONDUCT

"Laws control the lesser man; right conduct controls the greater one."

Mark Twain

Chapter 6

THE VALUE OF CHARACTER

GROWING UP IN Kenya, a certificate of good conduct was always very important. Every prospective new school or employer required a certificate of good conduct from your previous school or employer, and woe betide you if they did not provide you with one. It meant you would not be admitted into an institution or a new job. A certificate of good conduct was even more valued than your grades or skills. Why? Because no matter how educated or gifted you were, no institution or employer of worth would welcome you if your behaviour was bad.

Bad behaviour or lack of character negates your talent or skills, rendering them virtually useless as no one wants to be associated with you. The dictionary defines conduct as: "comporting oneself in a specified way, or how a person behaves especially in a particular situation or a mode or standard of behaviour especially about moral principles."

A person of good conduct is deemed one of good character. What then is character, and how does a person of good character present themselves?

Dictionary.com describes 'character' as "the aggregate of features and traits that form the individual nature of some person or thing." So it is who you are at your core, the values and beliefs you hold dear that direct your behaviour.

I believe character is who you are and what you do when no one is watching you. In other words, your behaviour is self-driven and not influenced by others. It means you do the right thing because you believe it is the right thing to do. A person of good character generally presents traits like integrity, honesty, courage, loyalty, fortitude, and other virtues. These character traits define who you are as a person and greatly influence the choices you make in your life. Thus, character is not limited to a single value but the cluster of traits you demonstrate in making good choices and avoiding bad ones. People with good character choose their moral values because they believe they are right.

Nowadays, moral values are trashed while popularity and charisma are elevated. What is popular has become more important than what is right. Truth is no longer valued while sensationalised falsehoods sell like hotcakes. You might ask, 'Why bother with the truth if it wins no brownie points?' It is also fair under modern circumstances to ask, 'What then is the value of a good character?'

Both classical and Biblical cultures believed that the health of a society is determined by the sum of the people's characters within them. Ralph Waldo Emerson[22], the 19th-century American philosopher and poet, said, "Men of character are the conscience of the society to which they belong." Without people of character, there could be no trust and justice in society and, thus, no community or stability.

Good character was highly rated in previous times but not so much today. In modern times, everything sells, and the celebrity culture that has become our way of life means people become famous more often for notoriety than genuine value. As a result, character is underrated, and young people in today's popular culture are doing anything to become famous without conscience. They call it freedom of expression but often do not link what they express to anything other than their passing whims and fancies. Morality and virtue do not factor into their equation for what is worth doing. They want to live their lives as they wish without regard for consequences.

They need to know that there is no freedom without values and character. Liberty is not the freedom to do just as we please; liberty is the freedom to do as we ought. We are all shapers of our community and as such, we should all be responsible for cultivating the character we need to contribute positively to our collective. We can do so by leading lives with values that inspire others and thus contribute to our communities.

Knowing what a good character looks like, how do we then develop it for ourselves? Ralph Waldo Emerson said, "Deciding to become a man of good character means choosing to live a more disciplined and less selfish life." One thing is for certain, nobody was born with a good character. Character is built and shaped over time. We were all born innocent but grew up being shaped by the environment that we grew up in. First, we learnt from our caregivers, who became our role models at home. Later, we were socialised into our communities and culture, then learned more through education and often religion. All these people and places instilled values and beliefs that made us who we are today.

Regardless of where you grew up and your beliefs, I believe we all know right from wrong. That is the core judgement on which good character is developed. Thus, anyone can become a person of character and we are all capable of building good character. However, we must add another factor to this capability: intention, supported by hard work and commitment to realise it.

When a person possesses good character, it is exhibited through their words and actions. Below are a few steps to help you on your journey to becoming a person of character.

Five Steps To Becoming A Person of Character

1. **Define your core values**

   Know what is most important to you by determining the values you want to uphold personally and professionally. The previous module on core values must have helped you to identify the core values you want to live by. For example, here are a few traits and values that make one a person of character: integrity, honesty, loyalty, kindness, courage, respect, responsibility, authenticity, self-discipline, optimism, and mindfulness, to name a few.

2. **Associate yourself with people of good character**

   Surround yourself with people of good character, people you want to emulate and learn from. Avoid people who make bad decisions. If you are not surrounded by such people, get a hero whose character you admire and wish to emulate. We have heroes like Nelson Mandela, Martin Luther King, Gandhi, Abraham Lincoln, etc. Decide who you have always admired. Study your hero's good characteristics, behaviours, and habits, then start emulating them.

3. **Follow and practise good habits**

    Once you have defined your core values and
    identified your hero's habits, study these habits
    and start practising them. Pick one or two from
    the list of positive character traits above to practise
    for several weeks. Write down the actions you want
    to take or the behaviours that reflect this trait and
    implement them in your daily life and interactions.

4. **Develop self-awareness of your thoughts, feelings
    and behaviours**

    Make it your normal practice to reflect on your
    behaviour and interaction with others. Make a habit
    of going through what happened, what you said and
    did, and why you took those actions. Also, review
    what informed, made, or drove you to do what you
    did or say what you said. This self-awareness and
    self-reflection exercise will greatly help you change
    and manage your behaviour, develop self-control,
    and help build your character.

5. **Endeavour to have a personal brand that defines you as a person**

Think legacy. How would you want family, friends or others who come across you to remember you? How would you want them to describe you? What would you want them to say about you when you are not present? How would you want people to feel when they interact with you? The great American writer Maya Angelou said: "People will forget what you said, people will forget what you did, but people will never forget how you made them feel." People of great character make others feel valued and treat them with humanity. Endeavour to treat others with respect.

MODULE 4: EMOTIONS

"Until you make the unconscious conscious, it will direct your life and you will call it fate."

Carl Jung

Chapter 7

MASTER YOUR EMOTIONS

IN PSYCHOLOGY, EMOTION is often defined as a complex state of feeling that causes physical and psychological changes, which in turn, influence thought and behaviour. Emotions are universal. Everyone, regardless of race, culture, or background, experiences emotions. Emotions make us human. Depending on the emotions we are experiencing, we communicate with each other in different ways, verbal or non-verbal. Emotions also help us protect ourselves by running or keeping away from danger and drive us to connect with one another. Emotions make us feel alive and help us stay alive. If we did not have emotions, we would be like robots, machines that take orders and act mechanically with no feelings. Emotions direct our behaviour; they act like data that signals us what to do in different circumstances. Emotions send us messages, and when we pay attention to their messages, we gather the motivation and energy to change things.

Emotions are inbuilt. They are generated subconsciously. They are autonomous bodily responses to certain internal or external events. This means an emotion can be generated from a thought (originating from within us) or an outside event (originating from our external environment). For example, the simple thought of presenting a speech in front of an audience (internal) can cause fear and anxiety, and a gunshot outside your house (external) can also generate fear. Emotions tell us something, send us signals, and when we pay attention to their messages or signals, we can gather the energy to take action and change things.

There are many alleged emotions, and researchers have different opinions about them. In this book, I will cite eight primary emotions indicated by Marsha Linehan[23] in her book, 'Dialectical Behaviour Therapy'

(DBT) Program. They are fear, joy, anger, sadness, interest, guilt, shame and disgust. Let us look at these emotions individually and see how they protect or inform us.

- Fear helps us keep away from danger. We all know that if you see a lion or other danger coming your way, fear makes you run for your life.
- Joy is infectious and makes us connect with other people.
- Anger indicates that we are being blocked from achieving a desired goal.
- Sadness is very useful in communicating to others that we feel distressed and need comfort and support.
- Interest elicits curiosity in us and can lead to creativity.
- Guilt and shame mainly remind us of our moral obligations, for example, how to behave and treat others. Thus, guilt and shame make us want to atone for our misdeeds and avoid behaviours that will cause us shame or guilt.
- Disgust protects us by keeping us away from toxic events like bad smells and potentially poisonous food.

Why Are Emotions Important?

Emotions are very important when it comes to our cognitive processes like perception, learning, memory, reasoning, and problem-solving. They have a strong influence on attention, especially modulating selective attention as well as motivating action and behaviour. For example, we know that tests, exams, homework, and deadlines can elicit fear, anxiety, and frustration. The same can be said that emotions also influence our ability to learn and remember. Thus, emotions have a pervasive impact on our lives and way of being.

We now appreciate how important and necessary emotions are for guiding, protecting, and aiding the attainment of our life goals. However, we should also be aware that emotions can cause pain, heartache, and damage or havoc in our lives and those of others if not managed well. Emotions are powerful; they can cloud your reason and make you do stupid, harmful, and destructive things you will regret later. Which of us has not fallen victim to emotions driving us into deeply regretful actions? There is a saying I like to follow, which reads, "Do not promise when you are happy, do not reply when you are angry, and do not decide when you are sad." Why? Because you might find that you were doing these things driven by emotions that, when they subside, you would realise you should not have done what you did.

Some emotions can be very painful and, if not appropriately managed, can adversely impact your mental well-being. In my experience, I classify anger, sadness, fear, shame, and guilt as dangerous to our mental well-being if not well managed. We all need to know and be aware of these emotions and, most importantly, learn how to manage them appropriately. However, learning how to manage other emotions we may not classify as 'red flag emotions' is still very important.

How Do We Manage Emotions?

Learning how to manage and regulate our emotions is critical. In the modern world, especially at work, people are no longer judged only by their academic or intellectual capabilities; they are judged and hired on how well they handle themselves and others. This ability is what Daniel Goleman[24] called emotional intelligence. Emotional intelligence is the ability to identify, manage, and regulate one's emotions and those of others. These are skills we were never taught in school. Nobody told us how important they are, but we all know that out-of-control emotions make clever and learned people appear foolish or inept. So the big question is, "How should we manage our emotions?" There are a few key skills that can help us to manage our emotions.

1. **Self-Awareness**

   Self-awareness is about being aware of what you are thinking, feeling, and doing in the present moment. Human beings are creatures of habit. We normally operate on autopilot, meaning we are not very consciously aware of what we are thinking, feeling, or doing. Start building emotional awareness by being consciously aware of what you are thinking, feeling, and doing in the present moment, being in tune with your body and mind. Being intentionally mindful and practising mindfulness can help you achieve this.

2. Know Your Emotions And How You Experience Them

For instance, be aware of what emotion you are experiencing. Can you name that emotion and where you are feeling it? In other words, what bodily sensations are the emotions triggering in you, and where are those sensations located?

Once you identify and label the emotion, can you trace it back to where and what caused it? What happened? Did someone say or do something to you? Did you hear, see, or do something yourself? Or what kind of thoughts were you having or thinking? Tracing the source is vital because emotions do not just happen. Emotions are caused by internal experiences (thoughts) or external stimulus or events. In short, what triggered that emotion? Learn and get into the habit of engaging yourself with this exercise and your self-awareness will grow.

Let's illustrate this with an example, say fear. First, identify the emotion and label it. Next, name the emotion; in this case, it is fear. What bodily sensations is it causing you to feel? Fear can result in chest pain, an elevated heart rate or palpitations, shaking or sweating. You might feel lightheaded, short of breath, or tingling or numbness in parts of your body. You could feel some or all of these sensations because everybody differs in how they experience body reactions. The severity of the emotion would also affect its associated bodily symptoms.

Now that you know you are experiencing fear, ask yourself what happened. What triggered this fear? What are you afraid of? What is causing this fear? Is the fear real or imagined? Once you identify the emotion and go through the above process, it helps you to be present and aware of yourself and what you are experiencing. This awareness and questioning go a long way towards lessening the effects of the emotion, allowing you to access your rational mind. In turn, your rational mind enables you to see things clearly, problem-solve, and make wise decisions instead of being paralysed by fear or driven to perform other non-productive behaviours.

3. Accept Your Emotions

Once you have identified the emotion, the next step is acceptance. Accepting the emotion means not running away from it or ignoring it. Instead, try and sit with that emotion, difficult as it is, and try to tolerate it. Normally, the emotion should run its course (hit its highest point) and lose its intensity after some time. Accepting the emotion instead of running away from it takes the edge off the emotion and helps you feel in control rather than the emotion controlling you.

Emotions can be very painful, and often when we have an uncomfortable feeling such as fear, anger, sadness, guilt, or shame, our first reaction is to run away, to dissociate from, suppress, or reject that feeling. Often, we end up trying to get rid of the feeling by using drugs, alcohol, or engaging in other harmful habits or behaviours that make us feel better. Unfortunately, we can also act or react in a harmful way, like shouting or saying hurtful things or even end up doing something dangerous, like being violent towards or harming someone. Awareness and acceptance of our emotions give us time to reason and access our wise mind.

We have all experienced intense and strong emotions and know what happened and the consequences of our actions. Sometimes, reactions to a primary emotion can lead to or generate a second, third and even fourth emotion. Before you know it, you are in a maelstrom of emotions. People frequently describe this as feeling mixed emotions. These emotions are called secondary emotions. For example, you can get into an argument with someone, leading to anger. From anger, you hit the person (reaction), leading you to experience regret and guilt, which can also move to shame. Thinking of the consequences of your behaviour (hitting) leads to fear and sadness. Now, you end up with a group of emotions and cannot tell what you are feeling or experiencing. Thus, your thinking, behaviour, and decision-making process get affected leading to an unhealthy state of being that can compromise your mental and emotional health. During these kinds of states, people do stupid things, which is why it is important to manage that first primary emotion or simply be aware of what your emotions are and what is happening to you.

As a mental health practitioner, I have observed that people start to ideate suicide during episodes of turmoil or intertwined emotions. They do things in a confused state with a complete lack of self-awareness as they react to the situation. They are in this state because they do not want to face what they are feeling and are not mindful or aware of how they are. Such can be the impact of emotions that are felt so strongly they seem overwhelmingly painful. Professional experience has also revealed that self-harming is another mechanism people use to cope with painful emotions.

Ironically, our lack of emotional awareness drives us to be led by them. That is what we call being in an 'emotional mind.' With the example above, you can see how emotionally driven behaviours create havoc and problems in our lives and, in most cases, result in unwise decisions. Marsha Linehan describes three types of minds: emotional, rational, and wise. However, the battle is usually between the emotional and rational minds. These two minds are very important and have their place in our daily lives. There are times when the emotional mind is needed, like when in love and experiencing or expressing a romantic or inspirational moment. In contrast, the rational mind is useful when analysing a problem or when a surgeon is operating on a patient.

Albert Einstein believed that true wisdom requires you to tap into both the emotional and rational minds (See Figure 2).

The Emotional mind is being in an emotional state where you experience raw and emotion-driven thoughts and behaviours. These emotions are hot, feelings-focused, intense, and volatile. In this state, you end up doing things without thinking of the consequences. For example, if you are angry with someone, you get angry thoughts of hurting them or retaliating, and you can even end up carrying it out. On the positive side, emotions are great for sparking inspiration, highlighting important values, and fuelling actions.

The Rational mind is where you think rationally and logically. Here, you are thinking clearly, dealing with reality, and seeing things as they truly are. You are dealing with the facts. The rational mind is cool, task-oriented, logic-focused, and pragmatic. It is great for making careful decisions, analysing facts, and solving problems, for example, mathematical problems. However, being in the rational mind all the time can make you appear boring and emotionless (robotic). The rational mind is mainly needed when solving problems.

The Wise mind is an integration of both emotional and rational minds. It acknowledges the role of emotion in pointing out what is important and uses reasoning to implement effective actions. It is intuitive, grounded, and mindful. Your "wise mind" is the intersection of your rational and emotional minds, allowing you to make the most grounded, useful, and fulfilling life choices.

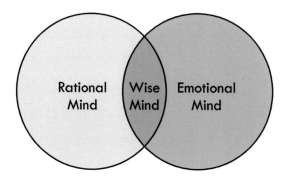

Figure 2: The Wise Mind. Adapted from Marsha Linehan's 'Dialectical Behaviour Therapy' book.

Being self-aware about your thoughts and feelings in the present helps you activate your wise mind by paying attention to both emotions and reasoning. It enables you to take your time with integrating them and making wise decisions. Please note we cannot always be in our wise mind, but developing self-awareness will help you improve and make the right decisions in the moment.

Understanding And Decoding
The Emotions of Others

The ability to decode emotions is a basic social skill. Accurately reading other people's emotions plays a key role in social interactions. We do this by observing and listening to others. Other people's body language, like facial expressions and tone of voice, should inform you about their emotions. There are three different ways to read other people's emotions. These are by observation, talking, and listening. Knowing whether the people you are with are happy, angry, fearful, or sad will help you gauge your interactions with them.

It is very important to be aware of what you are feeling and what others are feeling. Be observant of others, whoever they are. It could be family, friends, colleagues, or general members of the public. What are they feeling? Can you deduce their feelings by observing their behaviour, body language, facial expressions and what they say? Are you aware of or are you oblivious to others and their emotions? By asking what they are feeling, listening to what they are saying and what they are not (active listening), how they are saying it (volume and tone of speech), and observing their behaviour, body language and facial expressions, we can read people. By decoding other people's emotions, you are in a better position to connect with them, not only on a physical but emotional level as well. People aware of their own emotions and that of others are regarded as having a high emotional quotient (EQ)or emotional intelligence.

According to Dr Goleman, great leaders have a high EQ and Social Health. To be a great leader, you must have great self-control, which means being able to manage and regulate your emotions as well as read other people's emotions. Emotional intelligence distinguishes star performers from mediocre ones. Lack of awareness of other people's emotions causes you to be out of touch with others, thus making it difficult to have a good relationship with other human beings at work, at home, or in society. Focusing only on your own emotions and failing to decode others' emotions means you lack empathy, flexibility, and adaptability, making you look insensitive and self-centred. Once others form such an opinion of you, they will distance themselves from you, leading to loneliness, depression and unhappiness, and putting your social health at risk. You protect your social health by relating with others through your basic ability to decode their feelings and respond to them appropriately.

Here I would offer a word of advice regarding your boundaries of responsibility. Yours is to understand, empathise, and give support where you can, but you are not responsible for the emotions and reactions of others.

Identifying False Beliefs About Emotions

Take a moment to review your beliefs about emotions and your attitude to them. Do you have problems accepting and acknowledging your emotions? What were you taught about showing and expressing your emotions? We all have many false, distorted, and limiting beliefs buried in our subconscious, and they have influenced our attitude to life. Most of our false beliefs originate from our early childhood upbringing and environment.

In some cultures, people are taught or led to believe it is unacceptable to show or express emotion. So, they grow up believing that showing emotion is unacceptable or a show of weakness. These beliefs normally lead to the avoidance or dismissal of emotions. This attitude prevents the individual from developing self-awareness, self-understanding, and the ability to take care of themselves appropriately.

For example, owing to societal norms, beliefs, and expectations, most cultures seed the belief that men do not and should not cry. There is a common belief that it is not manly for men to show their emotions, except those portraying dominant behaviours. Men are deemed weak or labelled 'sissy boys', 'big girl's blouse,' or 'effeminate' if they display emotions that lead to non-dominant behaviours. Many men want to remain stoical, strong, and unmoved by what is happening around them, but this is wrong. It does not mean that they are not experiencing the emotions. No!

On the contrary, they feel emotions like any other human being, but they have to put up a front and function as if they are not feeling anything. Putting up a façade is more harmful than expressing emotions. Expressing one's emotions appropriately is not a weakness. Quite the contrary, it is strength. You are being authentic instead of denying and giving a false impression that you are not struggling inside. The emotional turmoil resulting from denying or attempting to hide our emotions damages our mental and physical health. Suppressed emotions cause long-term health problems.

Boys are normally taught at an early age not to show emotion and are chastised for crying or expressing themselves, especially those judged to show weakness. As a result, boys grow up to become men who hardly share or express their emotions to their families or friends. The major emotions men are societally permitted to show are those associated with anger, aggression, and dominance. They suppress emotions like sadness, fear, shame, or guilt. They believe by showing these emotions, they present themselves as unmanly. They do this because they have learned it is not okay to show vulnerability. It should therefore be no wonder that statistics show more men commit suicide than women. High suicide rates among men are believed to occur because men rarely share their emotional problems with others.

Things pushed under water have a way of bobbing back up to the surface. Suppressed emotions are no different. In his book 'When the Body Says No,' Gabor Mate[25,] a renowned expert on addiction, trauma, childhood development, and the relationship between stress and illness, explains how emotional stress is a major cause of physical illnesses, including cancer, auto-immune conditions and many other chronic diseases. He says the brain and body systems that process emotions are intimately connected by the hormonal apparatus, the nervous system, and the immune system. He talks about the considerable number of physical illnesses that are caused by suppressing emotions.

Suppressing emotions can also lead to suicide. Suicide happens when people cannot hold their suppressed emotions down anymore. Suppressed emotions may also cause a total mental breakdown. It, therefore, becomes crucial for the sake of our lives that we should endeavour to change these societal programs and wrong beliefs about emotions. Suppressed emotions are toxic and can kill or cause grave damage to your health. It is very right, healthy, and healing to express your emotions in a healthy way. We are all human beings, and one thing that makes us human is emotions; we should not be ashamed of them. I want to encourage men and other individuals who hold these false beliefs to shun them and start accepting and expressing their emotions in a healthy way.

Please know that you are not your emotions. Your emotions come and go like waves. Therefore, you should learn to ride the waves or currents akin to acceptance of the emotion. Also, remember that acceptance does not mean the process is not painful or difficult, nor does it mean it is fair to feel what you are feeling. It just means that you accept the emotion for what it is.

MODULE 5: PERCEPTION

"Change the way you look at things and the things you look at change."

Wayne W. Dyer

Chapter 8

PERCEPTION – EXPAND YOUR WORLDVIEW

L ET'S START BY asking what perception is. There is an old Indian fable told of six blind men who had never seen an elephant. Curious to know what an elephant looked like, they asked to be led to one so they could feel with their other senses than sight what it looked like, and they got their wish.

The first blind man touched the side of the majestic animal and declared with conviction that an elephant was smooth and solid like a wall. The second unsighted man touched the pachyderm's trunk and described the elephant as a giant snake. The third of the six men touched and felt the large, pointed tusks, quickly concluding that an elephant is as dangerous as a great spear. The fourth blind man touched the elephant's four solid legs and decided the creature must be a large cow-like animal. The fifth blind man touched the elephant's giant flapping ears, and he likened the elephant to a large, cooling fan. Finally, the sixth of our visually impaired observers was somewhat disappointed to have to report the elephant as a thick rope after feeling only its tail. After they touched the elephant, they sat together to discuss the appearance of an elephant based on their respective conclusions after touching and feeling six distinct parts of its body. Each of the blind men was emphatic and confident about the appearance of an elephant based (entirely) on the body part of the animal each had touched.

There Is a moral to this story. Humans think and claim they know or hold the truth based on their limited subjective experience. They tend to discount other people's subjective experiences, which may be just as true from their perspective. The story implies that while one's experience and opinion can be true on any subject, the level of truth and insight those experiences provide are partial and not the entire truth. One needs to look at every phenomenon holistically and see it from multiple perspectives to gain a more accurate picture of reality.

Priming, Previous And Current Experiences

We interpret our environment with reference to our own lived experiences. Thus, our previous knowledge and experiences prime us to interpret phenomena in particular ways unique to us and based on them. A person who grew up in a hot tropical climate will think of images like fans when describing the big flappy ears of an elephant. If that person had grown up in a cold environment, they might think of a curtain or a shawl when describing the elephant's ears. Each person draws from their experience, which tends to prejudice our interpretation of external phenomena.

Limited Data And Holistic Data

The result of priming by past and current experience means that those six blind men could have argued forever, each claiming to know what an elephant looks like based on the limited data (subjective experience) of the part they touched and forgetting they all touched the same thing (holistic knowledge based on a larger data set). If you also look at their interpretation, they interpreted the parts they touched from what they already knew or had come across. For example, depending on the body part, the one who touched the ear compared it to a fan, the tail to a rope, and the tusk to a spear. We could also conclude that if these men had come from another part of the world, they would use different items to illustrate the appearance of an elephant.

At first, these six blind men had their own limited and prejudiced perception of what an elephant looked like based on their experience of touching a discrete part of it. The story ends with the six men sharing what they had learned. Putting the parts together helped them to have a holistic picture of an elephant's appearance.

Decision-making Based On Respecting Our Diversity
As human beings, our lives are fraught with problems within and without, often arising from how we perceive things. Although we are all equal in worth, we are different and present with different ethnicities, races,

creeds, appearances, and physical attributes. We were all raised in different environments, cultures, and religions and socialised in diverse ways. We all come with rich but different experiences and, therefore, will have our personal views and opinions on issues. Given this diversity of views and opinions, how can we agree and live harmoniously with each other?

The solution is to be aware and respectful of the differences in our backgrounds and perception. We also need to understand where the other person is coming from. We need to try and move to their side of the street and see issues from their perspective, explore how they feel, and then observe the world through their lenses. This is called 'perspective taking' or taking the other person's perspective. This approach will reduce arguments and tensions that plague our everyday relationships at home and work. We are all human beings. We live on the same planet, with untold potential, but we argue, disagree, fight, and kill each other due to our partial and limited experience of our universe. In short, our inability to engage in perspective-taking causes unnecessary conflicts.

A Definition of Perception

From the story above, we see that perception is the collection of information on the world and our interpretation and comprehension of that information. It is a process by which individuals organise and interpret their sensory impressions to give meaning to their environments. Perception is influenced by your personal characteristics, beliefs, and experiences. That is why two people can perceive the same thing differently.

The Perception Process

The perception process involves three steps: Selection, Organisation, and Interpretation of data. These steps help us organise and interpret the chaos of what we see, touch, taste, hear, and smell in our world.

Selection is deciding what to pay attention to. We are bombarded by data and stimuli the moment we wake up. We take in this data by using our five senses of sight, taste, touch, smell, and hearing. If we were to pay attention to all the data we are taking in, we would experience a sensory overload. Moreover, it is not every piece of information we need to advance our life goals. Thus, humans are biologically evolved to seek information that helps us avoid pain or danger first, then maximise pleasure and abundance. We rapidly select information that gives us cues to make decisions that advance our goals. We also use as little data as possible to speed up the decision-making process so that we can maximise our opportunities.

Organisation is a critical component of perception. Once the brain selects what to pay attention to, it organises the information by what sticks out first. When there is so much happening around us, we focus on what stands out the most. Consider being at an office Christmas party. Visually, you might pay attention to someone's dress or behaviour if they are strikingly smart, oddly dressed, or extremely drunk. Our ears might pick out loud people due to their jollity or antisocial behaviour. When it comes to taste, you might notice spicy, bland, or rich foods jumping out at you. In terms of touch, you could have felt the softness of the tablecloth or even the springiness of the carpet. With smell, it could be the perfume of somebody close to you in the room.

We interpret the sensory information we have collected based on our expectations of people in certain places and events. These expectations could be positive or negative depending on our past knowledge, experiences, and beliefs. For example, you are invited to the office party but expect it to be boring, judging by the lacklustre experience of the previous year. However, your perception could change after you attend the party and find it interesting. In addition, we create explanations for other people's behaviour based on their appearance, personality, status, gender, and prevailing racial stereotypes.

Changing Your Perspective For Better Communication And Relationships

Imagine being at work, sitting in the cafeteria during lunch, and seeing two or three colleagues talking to each other. A moment later, you turn around and catch them laughing while looking at you. As a result, you think they are laughing at you and conclude they have been talking about you. You then become resentful, snappy, angry, and withdrawn because you believe they are talking about you. Now, you do not have all the facts, so your perception could be wrong. Your interpretation of the event could be driven by your current relationship with the trio or one of them, past experience, problems at work, or even what you think about yourself. However, walking around with resentment and anger will not help you or promote teamwork. It will also not create a conducive working environment. Moreover, being unhappy at work is not healthy for you.

So, what do you need to do? The simple solution is to check your perception and determine whether it accurately reflects reality. For example, you might be surprised that the trio apparently laughing at you were laughing at something totally different. You just happened to make eye contact with them when they laughed.

Effective communication requires self-reflection, a better understanding of the perception process, and a commitment to change. Of course, that is easier said than done. However, with some practice, you can gain new insights into perceiving and navigating your world. Here are some guidelines for improving perception and communication with others:

1. **Avoid mind-reading**

   Issues in relationships are often caused by mind-reading. A classic example is when you walk around with resentment building up inside you for a perceived wrong your partner or friend did to you. However, you never asked, informed, or discussed the issue with your friend or partner, so they have no idea why you are upset. The problem is it is all built up in your mind. As in the workplace scenario, the best way to find out someone else's perception or point of view is to ask them directly.

2. **Distinguish between facts and inferences**

   A fact is an information that can be checked and verified. Inferences are assumptions made on facts but not necessarily an accurate meaning of these facts. Try to remember these differences, especially at work. For example, a company letter states that budget cuts are happening next quarter. Your co-worker immediately infers from the message that they will be fired. While the company budget cut is a fact, how the company will be affected has not been disclosed yet.

Any inferences made at this point will only be suppositions that could cause unnecessary stress and miscommunication.

3. **Monitor the labels you use**

    Labelling is a tool people use to understand the complexity of the world they struggle to interpret. However, labelling others, especially unconsciously, can cause long-term consequences and misunderstandings. For example, at work, we may label a co-worker as difficult. But shifting our thinking from 'This person is difficult' to 'I have difficulty with this person' changes how we view and relate with the colleague. Furthermore, labelling people can become toxic and unproductive. For example, numerous lives have been lost due to racially motivated behaviour by specific labels that justify aggression against the abused group.

4. **Always check your perception**

    Is it factual and real or imagined? Check the facts before making any conclusions. Repeating these processes and committing to change will help you become a better person and communicator and a better friend, partner, and co-worker.

Self-Perception

Self-perception is how you view yourself and your traits based on your thoughts, beliefs, and behaviours. There are two types of perception: how you see yourself and your world and how others see you and their world. You can only control your perception. How you perceive yourself and your world influences your attitude, which, in turn, affects what you attract. Perception is about what you pay attention to and how you interpret it. It is also about how you act on or react to it. If you perceive a world of abundance, your actions and attitude attract abundance. If you see yourself in a negative way, you get negative outcomes, but when you see yourself in a positive way, you get positive outcomes. Why? Because you will act according to the way you see yourself.

I am reminded of the Bible story of the twelve spies sent by Moses to scout the land of Canaan for forty days. Among the spies, only two were optimistic and believed they could fight and conquer the territory.

Ten others gave a negative report, stating that the people in the land were giants and compared with them, they were like grasshoppers. There was no way they could fight, defeat them, and conquer the land. Interestingly, the Bible says none of the ten lived to see Canaan. However, the positive two, Joshua and Caleb, lived to see the promised land and lived long after. Joshua and Caleb saw a fertile land worth fighting for and believed they could defeat the inhabitants of the land. They believed they were worthy and able, while the others considered themselves grasshoppers compared to the inhabitants of the land and believed otherwise. This shows the power of perception. It can stop you from becoming your best and cause conflicts, misery, unhappiness and lack of fulfilment in life. Be aware of your self-perception. How do you perceive yourself? If you perceive yourself mostly negatively, try and change that. Start seeing yourself in a positive light. Speak positive language like 'I can do it', 'It is possible', 'There is a way', etc. Have a positive outlook and pray for courage and strength.

.

MODULE 6: THOUGHTS

"Never underestimate the power of thought; it is the greatest path to discovery."

Idowu Koyenikan

Chapter 9

YOUR THOUGHTS ARE POWERFUL

A POPULAR QUOTE from the Bible reads: *"As he thinketh in his heart, so is he..."*[26] This passage never made sense to me until I became a mental health professional. It became even clearer when I read the book "As A Man Thinketh" by James Allen[27]. When I thought more deeply about the statement, I realised how true it is in life. In my work, I observed that we deal with the manifestations and results of people's thoughts. Whether it is depression, trauma, psychosis, or other serious mental illness all go back to the patient's thoughts and thought processes. It shows that our lives are driven by what and how we think on a habitual basis. We should all know this, but various factors prevent us from becoming aware of what we think about and how our thoughts influence our lives.

For a better understanding, let us consider the dictionary definition of a thought "an idea or opinion produced by thinking, or occurring suddenly in the mind. It can also be the action or process of thinking." According to Wikipedia, thoughts and thinking refer to conscious cognitive processes that can happen independently of sensory stimulation[28]. Thoughts manifest as judgements, reasoning, concept formation, problem-solving, and deliberation. However, thoughts encompass other mental processes such as ideation, memory, and imagination.

Unlike perception, thoughts occur internally and are independent of the sensory organs used to gather information about the environment. In its broadest sense, however, any mental event may be understood as a form of thinking, including perception and unconscious mental processes. Besides the mental processes, thoughts also refer to the mental states or systems of ideas brought about by these processes.

The Power of A Thought

From our discussion so far, we can deduce that thoughts are mainly ideas or concepts. Ideas create things and make things happen. Everything tangible and intangible we see or know emanates from a thought. By intangible, I mean things like alliances, movements, political parties or other philosophically attuned social engagements. Tangible things are physical, for example, chairs, cars, buses and aeroplanes. The idea that everything we see and use was once an idea in someone's mind is profound. Thus, our modern-day world is a result of the thoughts and ideas of people. All the wonderful and useful products, gadgets, and accessories were once in someone's head. They started life as an idea and eventually crystallised into substances we can see, use, and value. The mobile phone, computer, internet, aeroplane, trains, the dress or suit you wear are all end products of thoughts, and the list is endless.

Extend this concept to the universe or nature, and we can perhaps see that both started life in the mind or thoughts of the Creator, the divine intelligence behind the natural world and the unseen world. In the

Christian tradition, the Bible states that the Creator called each and everything into being. He called the oceans, seas, rivers, plants, and all other sentient and insentient things into existence, each with its purpose. He could not have called them into being if he had not thought about their appearance, how they would look and their intended purposes. Isn't that simply marvellous?

Our world has greatly changed due to the great ideas conceived and developed by its inhabitants. For example, the steam engine by Thomas Newcomen[29] in England in 1712 facilitated efficient transportation across the great continent, thereby revolutionising the American economy. The Wright brothers gave us the idea of powered flight, as did Henry Ford, the mass production of automobiles. In recent times, we have computers, mobile phones, and the Internet. These ideas have revolutionised how we live, work, socialise, and travel. So, what does this mean? It implies that thoughts become things, confirming their power to change history and our lives. We must therefore be deeply mindful of what we are thinking momentarily and daily.

Our minds churn out thousands if not millions of thoughts daily. What, then, are the kinds of thoughts you have daily? Are your thoughts creative ideas to solve problems, or are they useless and detrimental to you, your health and others? Some people worry about what others think about them, and some think about how they will hurt or take revenge on others. Others are filled with negative thoughts and ideas about themselves that do not create value. But, on the other hand, you find people who think of solving problems, developing ideas, and visualising the outcome. They work relentlessly on their ideas, even amid challenges, and bang! They eventually solve the problem and become celebrated.

What do you spend time thinking about? This question is important because you manifest what you think, hence the saying, "As A Man Thinketh, So Is He".

It is said that your thoughts can make you sick or heal you. Do you know that people with anxiety and depression suffer from their thoughts and imagination? They mainly suffer from thoughts of fear about what could happen, what people will say, what could go wrong, what will not work, etc. They envision worst-case scenarios. These thoughts and imaginations become so vivid and real that they start shaking with fear and develop anxiety and panic attacks which could lead to heart problems, high blood pressure, cardiac arrests, and other health issues.

Thoughts create emotions and emotions, in turn, create behaviours. Wayne Dyer[13], a renowned motivational speaker, said, "Change your thoughts, change your life." Why? Because your life reflects your thoughts. If you think negatively, your life will manifest negative outcomes and experiences. Think positively and you will manifest positive outcomes. Jim Rohn also said, "Stay guard at the door of your mind." He meant that you must be mindful of your thoughts and what you let into your mind all day. A Buddhist maxim posits, "One should become the master of his mind rather than let his mind master him."

We are taught in many traditions and philosophies to learn how to control our minds, i.e., our thoughts. Some people wonder why nothing ever works well for them, but if you think of failure, you will see and visualise failure. Most people are unaware of how powerful thoughts are, but the saddest thing is most people are not even aware of their thoughts, hence cannot form the connection between their thoughts and the state of their lives. The famous book, "Think and Grow Rich" by Napoleon Hill[30] says, "Your thoughts have brought you where you are." Think of that! You are where you are due to the quality of your thoughts.

So, what can you do? At the beginning of this book, I talked about the need to examine yourself by asking deep questions. At this point, the question is, where are you? What has brought you here? What kind of major decisions have you made in your life? What was the outcome or result of those decisions? Your decisions have brought you where you are. Decisions are the conclusions and actions you arrive at after the mental processes arising from your thoughts. Do a self-reflection and see how your thoughts have influenced or affected your life up to this point. The process of reflection will help you decide whether to change your thinking.

Three Steps To Mindful Thinking

What steps should you take to make your thoughts count and add to your life?

1. **Become aware of your thoughts**

   Do this daily, and moment by moment. How? By being intentionally mindful of what you are thinking about. Make a point of becoming self-aware of your thoughts. If you recognise you have negative, unhelpful or unproductive thoughts, change to positive thoughts or direct your thoughts to more useful thinking or imagination. You can change your thoughts by changing your activities, meditating, praying, or repeating a positive mantra or affirmation.

2. **Stand guard at the door of your mind**

   Be aware of what you let into your mind. Remember, our mind churns thousands of thoughts in a day. Thoughts emanate largely from our environment, memory, or what we see, feel, hear, taste, and touch. This means for our mind to think pleasant or great thoughts, we should surround ourselves with pleasant surroundings or environments conducive to motivating and enhancing our thinking patterns and processes. For example, what kind of people do you surround yourselves with? What kind of books do you read? What kind of movies or programmes do you watch? What are you exposed to in your daily life?

Someone said poor people talk about other people, rich people talk about things, and wealthy people talk about ideas. Which category of people do you hang around with? If you read about the Wright brothers, you will find that Wilbur, one of the brothers, spent most of his time reading in the library, and he and his brother ran a newspaper business. This means they were well-informed and abreast of what was happening in the world. It is more than likely their idea of an aeroplane was born out of what was happening then. It was the age of aviation. What are you feeding your mind with? What is the staple food of your mind? Your ideas and thoughts will be born from what you surround your mind with, what you feed and expose it to.

3. **Check your experiences and beliefs**

Your life experiences and beliefs can inform your daily thoughts and thinking patterns. Suppose you were brought up in an environment where you were constantly told you are stupid, foolish, and will never amount to anything, and you believed it. In that case, likely, you would not admit or let in thoughts of positive possibilities in your mind. You may reject any great thought or idea before it starts to form, thus closing the door to great possibilities because of the belief that you are not capable or worthy of them. These are called limiting beliefs. So, check what kind of beliefs you hold and where they came from, and start challenging them because you can think better, believe better, and move on to greater possibilities.

There are many stories of people who overcame adversity because they dared to think differently and believed they could do better. They decided nobody would dictate who they were or their place and what they could do or become, and they broke barriers to become who they wanted to be. What is holding us back from becoming who we are meant to be is our thoughts, beliefs, lack of a burning desire, faith, and persistence.

You are one thought, one idea away from changing your life!

MODULE 7: ACTION

"What we plant in the soil of contemplation, we shall reap in the harvest of action."

Meister Eckhart

Chapter 10

ACTION FOR RESULTS

THIS BOOK IS filled with stories, experiences, and knowledge. This is just information. We live in an age when information is abundant. We can also find millions of self-help books on making life easier and better. Information like this helps us learn about many subjects and issues. Knowledge without action yields no results. Only when we act on the knowledge gained can we have transformation. When we change on the inside, the world around us also changes. Action is, therefore, the key to unlocking great potential and transforming the world.

One definition of action is the process or state of acting or being active. Another is the fact or process of doing something, typically to achieve an aim implying that action must be with intent. It must be planned and put into play to achieve a goal or outcome. My book and program emphasise action as the key to manifesting your best self.

Often, people wonder why nothing changes in their lives, why they are unfulfilled or why a certain problem persists. They convince themselves they are doing something by gathering more information. Sometimes they lose track of their learning, so they gather more knowledge on the same subject, promising to do something this time. Ultimately, they procrastinate and never act despite having all the tools and processes to resolve their problems.

Some people start taking action, find the process painful or uncomfortable and give up. They return to their comfort zone even when it causes misery and pain. Let's take weight loss as an example. There is no doubt the individual is overweight and suffering serious health problems. They know they need to lose weight, and they have all the nutrition and exercise information. Nonetheless, they postpone exercising or go once or twice, which causes their muscles to ache, elevates their heart rate, makes them tired, and they quit. They cannot handle the pain and inconvenience of dieting and exercising. So they return to their usual routine with their weight problem firmly in place.

It is common in my profession to see a client move from one therapist to another or be in therapy for years, finally saying it doesn't work. I always tell my clients that therapy works when they work the therapy. Many clients believe therapists will work magic for them to get well. In talk therapy, they believe all they need to do is sit on the couch, talk, and magically get better. While talking is one way of alleviating emotional distress, talking alone will not solve problems. The client must apply and practise the skills and tools learned in therapy to inform and change their lives. In other words, a therapist is only there to guide, but the hard work is on the client to get results. It's like going to the doctor for a headache, being prescribed some medicine, and then refusing to take it. Would that headache be relieved? Of course not! However, if the headache persists after using the medication, you can return to the doctor, who can prescribe a stronger medication or run more tests. Likewise, you cannot expect results without practising the skills taught or following instructions during therapy sessions.

This example illustrates that no change can occur without action. A great idea, concept or thought can only be brought to life by implementing it. Otherwise, it remains nothing more than an idea in your mind. Myles Munroe[15] famously said, "the cemetery is rich with ideas that were never implemented, books that were never written, music that was never sung and inventions that never saw the light of day."

Why Some Ideas Never Come To Light

Self-doubt: not believing in yourself.

Fear of failure: not wanting to fail.

Stories you tell yourself: 'I can't do it', 'I am not worth it', 'I am not of that class', 'It is not possible'.

Procrastination: putting off action until another day that may never come.

Pain or discomfort: the pain **and** inconvenience of taking action.

Overcoming The Barriers To Action

To overcome the barriers to action, you need to 'JUST DO IT' as in the NIKE brand slogan or simply "JUST TAKE ACTION". Don't rationalise or analyse the situation so you don't talk yourself out of action. Instead, jump in and get it done.

Forget about your self-doubt, do not think about failing, and do not listen to the voices and stories you create in your head. Do not put it off or think about the pain it will cause. Instead, "JUST DO IT."

However, I would not be writing this if 'just doing it' was that easy for everyone. If it were that easy, we would all see and celebrate success in all areas of our lives. Unfortunately, this is not the case; most people remain stuck, miserable, sick, unfulfilled, broken and unhappy. Some of us are one action or a few actions away from fulfilling our dreams. Others need only to reject their false logic designed to maintain the status quo and courageously take action that will change their lives forever.

The action required depends on the problem and the desired outcome. Some problems, ideas and solutions just need one stroke of action and are solved. Other problems require repeated steps or a series of actions before achieving the desired results. You may need to go through multiple steps and processes before achieving the intended results. This implies that you have abundant patience, resources, resourcefulness, resilience, courage, strength, hope and faith to accomplish the goal. Unfortunately, many people lack these ingredients and give up easily on their dreams.

As discussed in the previous chapter, everything starts with a thought. The thought is then driven by desire and belief that you can do it. Next comes planning, and finally, implementation. For example, say you want to build a house. You'll first think of the kind of house you want to build (design, size, number of rooms, bathrooms, colour, garden space). Next is planning - putting the idea of the house you have in mind on paper, getting an architect to sketch and draw up the plans for you, or simply sketching it on paper. Then you consider the materials needed and the labour involved, with all costs within your budget. You will need to source the materials and then implement the plans. The result is a beautiful house.

It is now tangible and real from the idea through to its completion, ready for habitation because of the actions taken. If you just had an idea of a house and never acted on it, there wouldn't be a house.

In our case, if the previous chapters of this book have inspired you to desire change, become better or excel at what you do, then put the knowledge into action, and you will be guaranteed results.

Chapter ll

WINNING WHERE OTHERS HAVE FAILED

WHEN YOU WANT remarkable results, there are a few things you can do to make them possible. If you ask high achievers what they did to achieve their goals, they will tell you the following:

1. **Commitment**

   Commitment is essential for success. It is defined as a promise to do or give something. Commitment is choosing to do something and following through until results are achieved. Commitment will often call you to a greater sense of purpose. However, it demands that you remain determined to follow through on your decision. A commitment that is not completed is no commitment at all. It is better not to commit than to make one and not see it through to the end. Abraham Lincoln said, "Commitment transforms a promise into a reality". So, whether you want to lose weight, finish college or whatever you want, do not stop until you see it through. Throughout this book, I invite you to commit to becoming a better person and your excellent self. I believe there is no greater goal to commit to than this. When you make a commitment, especially to yourself, you strengthen your mind in ways that open up new possibilities. Once you have made a commitment, the next ingredient you need is self-discipline.

2. Self-Discipline

Discipline is setting up rules to shape behaviour. It means repeatedly following a specific set of rules to achieve your desired goal. Self-discipline is the ability to do the things that need to be done or control and train one's conduct. It is about self-restraint, ignoring distractions and controlling impulses.

158

As human beings, we are easily distracted. We prefer pleasure and avoid pain. We are also easily tempted and fail to achieve our goals, like the student who prefers to sleep or party rather than study for their exam. Self-discipline is critical because it shapes us and helps us focus on our goals and ignore and control impulsive responses that obstruct our goals.

With self-discipline, you set rules and create new habits, routines, and automatic mechanisms that help you order and manage your time and actions towards your goal. A good example of an automatic mechanism is Mel Robbins' 5-second rule[31]. The 5-second rule is a fantastic way to boost your motivation when you feel unmotivated to do something. Using the rule is simple. Start by counting backwards to yourself: 5-4-3-2-1. Counting will help you focus on the goal or commitment and distract you from worries, thoughts, and fears in your mind. As soon as you reach "1," move. That's it. Use the rule whenever you feel hesitant about doing something you should do.

I have listened to elite athletes and footballers.

One thing they will tell you is that they do not miss their daily exercise routine. Most successful people have habits and routines. They usually wake up early, follow the same daily routines, and maintain certain diets and food regimens. They will also tell you they follow this routine whether they like it or not. I urge you to create your own habits and set daily routines as part of your personal self-discipline protocols. In her book 'The 5-second Rule', Mel Robbins says that we cannot control how we feel but can control how we act. I remember when my son was in the hospital. Most days, all I wanted to do was stay under the duvet, cry and feel sorry for myself, but I would go against this impulse, ignore the feelings and rise from the duvet, get washed, dressed and ready to go to the hospital to be with my son. I TOOK ACTION!

3. Consistency

Next, we must be Consistent. The dictionary defines consistency as acting in a particular way no matter the circumstances. Consistency is the act of following certain steps over and over again to achieve a goal. It is all about creating a habit of investing in constant efforts to make incremental progress. For example, you want to learn to play the piano. At first, it is very difficult to master the keys, but once you consistently put in the effort and keep learning and playing the keyboard, you eventually become proficient in playing the piano. Consistency is the key to success.

The first attempt at anything can be difficult and might not yield results. It might even cause pain or embarrassment, and most people give up easily at this stage. However, with constant effort applied regularly without fail, your actions yield results. Most successful people understand the power of consistency, developing habits and following routines that become second nature. Most often, success does not depend on great talent but on dedicated effort over a long period. The quote "Genius is 1% inspiration and 99% perspiration" is attributed to Thomas Edison, the prolific American inventor who gave us the light bulb. He emphasised the importance of persistent effort and action for success. Likewise, for a piano player, the first keyboard strokes and occasional trials may sound appalling and discordant. Yet by constantly practising and playing the keyboard, you become proficient and eventually master the keyboard to become a great piano player. To manifest consistency, you need patience, belief and commitment. They say success is the sum of small efforts repeated day in and day out. Be consistent.

4. Persistence

The Dictionary defines persistence as the quality that allows someone to continue doing something or trying to do something even though it is difficult or opposed by others. Great goals or achievements take work to attain. Even with commitment, consistency and long hours of hard work, it can sometimes feel weary, and the goal might seem unachievable. This could be because of the challenges you encounter along the way. Challenges that were not expected or just due to the nature of the task or the problem you want to solve.

Thomas Edison invented the light bulb, but most need to learn that it took him 2,744 failed attempts before he got his working bulb. He is credited with more patents than any American ever, with over 1000 patents. Many assume the inventions came easily to him. They didn't. Moreover, he did not have an elite education, having been home-schooled by his mother because he did not get on well at school. He was also partially deaf. That is why he said genius is 1% inspiration and 99% perspiration. The work, time and effort might seem too much, and yes, it can be frustrating and demoralising, and many would want to quit.

As it was for Edison, there are times when things do not go according to plan, times when everything goes wrong and we fail. It is at such moments that you most want to give up. Most people indeed suffer from reduced confidence and self-esteem, making them feel bad about themselves when things go wrong. When this happens, we usually want to quit and do something easy or fun to distract us from the goal-oriented task. It is the natural human tendency to do the easy and fun things over those that are hard but necessary. Unless this mindset is changed, it can sadly lead to failure in life.

Persistence is required to achieve any worthy goal. If you read the history of any great person who accomplished a great feat, you always find that they had to overcome challenges. Still, despite the barriers and challenges encountered, these people showed tenacity. In other words, they never gave up. They showed persistence and eventually overcame the difficulties and won. The truth is greatness is realised by overcoming barriers. Any worthy goal presents challenges, and you will win only by persistence and deciding not to give up.

I am reminded of so many people who persisted with their dreams and goals and, as a result, became victors. They became great heroes for all time like Thomas Edison, who had to try over a thousand times before he got his light bulb right; the Wright brothers, pioneers of Aviation who never gave up despite people laughing at them; and Ford, who never gave up on the car engine that he wanted to produce. More recently, Steve Jobs gave us Apple and its range of record-beating smartphones and computers. Despite failing and encountering challenges, these people never gave up.

One thing I find common to all of them is that they believed in themselves and were committed to achieving their goals. They were persistent in the pursuit of their dreams. These people and many other heroes of past and present times teach us that we should never give up, even in the middle of difficulties. Instead, we must persist until we get what we want. "Only when it is dark enough can you see the stars," states an old proverb.

5. Diligence

Diligence is defined as careful and persistent work or effort. Put another way, diligence is hard work that is attentive to detail and minutiae. It is a universal truism that nothing comes from nothing, and hard, attentive work is required for any great results to be realised. Of course, hard work is never popular. Everybody wants to get things the easy way without toiling and sweating for it. It is becoming part of modern culture that we require and seek instant gratification. That is a situation in which our goals are achieved literally on demand. Life or nature is not like that. There is no effect without a cause and no result without action, consistency, persistence and diligence. It is simply a universal law of life. There is an apocryphal saying: 'NO PAIN, NO GAIN!' which means nothing of value comes with ease. Any good or beautiful thing needs to be worked on or worked for.

In the Bible, laziness and idleness are abhorred. 2 Thessalonian 3:10 says, "The one who is unwilling to work shall not eat." Man cannot live without work, and hard work gives results. Hard work is just that, HARD WORK! It can be hard, painful, frustrating, and may yield results only after some time, but the results will come. In the Catholic canon, sloth, defined as "a habitual disinclination to exertion, or laziness," is considered one of the seven deadly sins leading to man's downfall. Yet hard work alone is not enough. Hard work needs to be righteous and directed towards a goal. That is why I use diligence instead of plain hard work. Diligence implies careful, as opposed to haphazard, and persistent work or effort. Please note the word 'careful'. Although hard work brings results, you can work hard and still not obtain the desired results. In northern England, there is the expression that calls unharnessed and unregulated work the work of a "busy fool". We should be effective, not foolish, in directing our efforts and work. Also, hard work may even be unjust or corrupt, however hard it is. We should act within the law to maintain our reputation. Corrupt work will ultimately lead to failure when it is uncovered. Being diligent here means being careful, smart, thoughtful and truthful, meticulous and just in your work.

Being diligent would also be indicative of a good work ethic. A strong work ethic is important for achieving goals. A work ethic is a set of moral principles a person uses to guide their work behaviour. A good work ethic fuels one's needs and goals and is considered a source of self-respect, satisfaction and fulfilment. Diligence is one of the seven capital virtues, popularly known as remedial to the seven deadly sins. In Christianity, diligence describes the thoroughness, completeness, and persistence of action, particularly in matters of faith. In Buddhism, diligence leads to liberation, and its practice brings an increase in beneficial qualities. Thus, faith, the very practice of the religion, is described as assiduous, which means correct in detail, diligence and attitude. In Islam, it is said that a man has nothing but what he strives for, and that diligence brings fruits to sight. The fruits refer to the fruits of one's labour.

Nowadays, there is a celebrity culture where everyone wants to become a 'celeb' or an 'overnight success'. It is a culture where our young people want things to happen now! If they want it, they must have it now! The mainstream and social media have not made things easier either. Instant stardom, and huge attention from massive social media followings, sometimes in the millions, enable people to become hugely popular for creating little value. Popularity could derive from simply being 'cute', looking good or being outrageous. This has made young people today ignore the fundamentals of a fulfilling life. Modern celebrity culture negates the importance of hard work, learning, failing and getting up again, and going through the necessary processes to achieve something worthwhile. They do not know that those processes create patience, a great virtue. It is all about instant gratification, as mentioned above. Some call it 'fame in a microwave' that's cooked up very quickly. Celebrity culture is not only affecting young people; it is also evident in the wider society. People want to 'get rich quick' and therefore seek shortcuts that end up hurting and ruining other people's lives and sometimes their own.

We have corrupt leaders worldwide. The disclosure of government contracts for pandemic supplies has shown that many well-connected people profited from public funds at the expense of ordinary citizens. In world finance, we have people like Bernie Madoff, who started Ponzi and Pyramid Schemes that hurt and bankrupted many people leaving some homeless. He served a jail term of 150 years in prison, where he died. People engage in unethical behaviours to pursue fame, self-enrichment, and the lust for power and influence. Simply said, diligence pays handsomely and safely with your reputation intact.

6. Passion

I understand passion as a kind of energy, an emotion or a driving force that keeps you going regardless of the hurdles you encounter on your journey to achieve your goal. It is that thing that fuels you when you feel depleted and pushes you to do what is required to obtain your prize. When you want to become better or achieve a great goal, passion is that emotion which pushes you through, no matter what. A good example is when Christ endured pain and suffering on the cross to fulfil his desire to save humanity. We also have other heroes who endured much pain, discomfort and inconvenience in pursuit of a great goal. For example, Nelson Mandela was passionate about fighting apartheid in South Africa; the same could be said about Martin Luther King in his great fight for civil rights in America and Mahatma Gandhi, who had a passion to free India from British control with his non-violent movement that set India alight.

In our everyday lives, passion increases self-confidence and creativity and helps us overcome the difficult hurdles we encounter in pursuit of our goals. Nothing is as miserable as working in a job you are not passionate about or doing something you are not interested in. The effort becomes ten times harder, boring, and depressing, and you hate it. You lose the energy, motivation and desire to complete the task. No wonder many people are unhappy in their jobs, always waiting for the weekends to gain a reprieve from the drudgery.

When you are passionate about what you do, you do it effortlessly. You feel less pain. Even the obstacles inflate your desire to achieve your goals. Passion is the only way Edison could have stayed with his task despite the failures of his early light bulb designs. It is the only way Mandela could have survived a quarter century in jail. It is the only way Martin Luther King could have endured the billy clubs they beat him with at the demonstrations and marches in Selma, Alabama. During this journey of self-discovery, I urge you to infuse passion in your life and in the actions you take.

MODULE 8: NEW YOU

"Change can be scary, but you know what's scarier? Allowing fear to stop you from growing, evolving, and progressing."

Mandy Hale

Chapter 12

HAPPY NEW YOU!

A<small>T THE BEGINNING</small> of every year, we hear statements like 'NEW YEAR, NEW ME.' These words show the desire to change or do something better and new. Your desire could be to change your weight, relationships, lifestyle or behaviour. Whatever you intend to change, there is an understanding that you must do something different to bring the change. Jim Rohn, a respected motivational speaker, said, "For things to change in your life, you have to change, and you cannot live better without seeking to become better." Einstein's quote further supports this thought: "Insanity is doing the same thing repeatedly and expecting to get different results."

In the previous chapter, I discussed the importance of intentional action to achieve your desired goal. Action is the key to transformation. Once you act, things happen and you become a new person.

So, when you accept yourself fully and
- become confident of who you are,
- discover your core values and start living by them,
- shape your brand by building your character,
- become emotionally intelligent,
- change your perception and master your thoughts, you will experience change.

You do not have to follow the steps in this book sequentially; you can start with any module. The steps are intertwined and fluid, such that by addressing one aspect of the ACCEPTANCE framework, you produce transformation in other areas. A NEW YOU emerges as you continue to take action on the first six modules. You will start to think and feel differently about yourself and the world around you. Your behaviour will change, and you will begin to shift paradigms. You become attracted and interested in the things that are right for you. You may change the type of TV programmes you watch or watch no TV at all. You will start reading different books, attending growth seminars, seeking new relationships and friends, and exploring new interests. You will become more tolerant, no longer reacting to trivial matters that do not factor into your new life. You will also become more discerning, self-assured and less worried about what people say or think about you. You'll spend time on things that matter to you and enjoy your company.

These changes will begin from the inside as you ask yourself difficult and important questions about your life and become honest with yourself. You will question some long, firmly held beliefs and overcome unfounded fears. Finally, you will face the truth about yourself and feel liberated. Although the change might initially seem unsettling, 'A NEW YOU' is being born.

Birthing is always challenging. Imagine the struggle a newborn undergoes when entering this life. After nine months in a warm, dark womb, where all your needs are automatically met, it feels alien to burst into a new world with strange lights, smells, sounds and textures. There is much to learn, yet the rewards are extraordinary and boundless. You are given the opportunity to make your mark in a world whose language you did not even speak when you appeared in it. I use this analogy for you to appreciate the magnificence and achievement of birthing your new you. It will require significant effort and greatly impact your growth.

When I started on my journey to self-discovery and purpose, I asked the same questions discussed at the beginning of this book. Questions such as Who am I? What is my purpose on this planet? Who do I want to become? How would I like my life to be? These questions were triggered mainly by the loss of my son. I could not understand why a loving God took my son and left me behind, separating us. Ruminating on these questions led me to start a movement to change the status quo regarding stem cell registration and donation. I strongly felt that our people needed to know about the dire need for potential stem cell donors from the African community in the stem cell registry. Therefore, the Kevin Kararwa Leukaemia Trust[32] was founded to create this awareness to increase the number of potential stem cell donors and avoid losing more lives like Kevin's.

The desire to make a difference prompted the need to articulate my message and the self-awareness I had to improve my public speaking skills. What followed was my taking action to address this need. I remember browsing the internet and seeing a speaker, Andy Harlington, demonstrate how to do a presentation. He offered a full-day seminar on how to present without notes. Although I was sceptical, I attended anyway. At the end of the seminar, I paid for a 4-day programme on public speaking. Before then, I never thought I could pay over £2,000 for a 4-day programme. Never! That was money I did not have and had to fund with my credit card. It shows how hungry I was to change and improve that area of my life. Looking back, I realise that was one of the few signs I was changing.

I used to burn the midnight oil reading fiction books in the past, but that also changed. I started reading autobiographies and self-improvement books. My first two books in the new genres were 'The Purpose Driven Life' by Rick Warren[33] and Stephen Covey's[34] '7 Habits of Highly Effective People'. I stopped watching soap operas like EastEnders and would instead watch and listen to motivational speakers and evangelical ministers such as Joyce Meyer[35], T. D. Jakes[36], and Ravi Zacharias[4]. My new actions started changing my thinking, shifting my inner paradigms, beliefs and self-doubts. Eight years later, I am still on the journey to improve myself. I am yet to arrive, but I am far from where I started. I have changed in myriad ways. I can now confidently address a room full of people. However, the most crucial change is the inner change in my being, manifesting as resilience and emotional well-being. Most importantly, I feel at peace with who I am and happy with who I am becoming. Now, I have written this book which you are reading. I never thought I would write a book, but here it is!

Change does not come easy, especially if you have experienced rejection, childhood traumas, lack of good role models and cheerleaders. Some people have had traumatic childhood experiences or undergone other difficult experiences. Some have been raised in hugely dysfunctional families and have deeply held negative beliefs, self-doubt and fears. Navigating these issues in the journey of self-discovery is not a small feat and comes with pain and frustration. Hence, you must be determined and committed to the process if you want to improve and move from where you are. Whether it is about healing yourself from the past, relationships, financial situation or career, the process is not without its uncomfortable moments. Always remember the expression 'NO PAIN, NO GAIN'. You must focus on the main goal: becoming better, achieving more, being happier, being fulfilled, finding your purpose and so on. Whatever it is, visualise your future. What do you desire to be like in the next 5, 10 or 20 years? Who would you want to become? Where would you like to be? What would you like to achieve? What legacy would you like to leave behind? Once you focus on these aspirations, you will do what it takes and keep on striving to become better in the process.

On this journey, I have often felt like returning to my cocoon or being my old self. I have felt like quitting or doing the minimum to survive – work, home, eat, TV, friends, sleep, and church, nothing more. But I kept growing by reading more books, meeting new people, attending more seminars and conferences, and watching useful content online. These activities fed my mind with what I wanted to manifest, and I kept doing them. The stimuli you expose yourself to can motivate you to grow or leave you where you are, sometimes even making you more negative. However, I feel better and more purposeful after exposing myself to useful content.

I firmly believe I was not meant to appear on the planet and just exist. I have a purpose, and for that one reason, I know I matter. This makes me feel worthy, different than before and happier with myself. But I also see if I go back to my old habits, which were not helping me to grow, I will be miserable. So, there is no point in going back there.

Sometimes, you might feel you are doing well when, out of the blue, BANG! Something happens, and you find yourself relapsing to your old self, old behaviours and negative thoughts and fears. Also, things might not work out fast as you strive to become this new person or achieve your desired goal, which might bring frustration and make you feel like quitting. But, please, do not give up on yourself. Wake up, dust yourself off, forgive yourself and persist in becoming the NEW YOU. The NEW YOU will be positively different from your former self in so many ways, so you might end up not even recognising yourself. The best thing is that you will continue to grow to greater heights because growth is continuous.

Here is a word of caution. Be aware that when you start changing and becoming this new person, your family, friends, and tribe will notice the difference, and they might be the first people to oppose your transformation. Their opposition may shock you. They might tell you words like "You are now so full of yourself" and "Who do you think you are?" "Do you think you are special?"

You also might struggle with doubts as you find yourself alone and not fitting in with the old 'besties.' You may experience feelings of guilt as you turn your back on the old culture, saying NO to unproductive habits or activities you used to do with friends. Also, you might experience a period of loneliness and isolation as you find your place in this journey. Feelings of not belonging to the New Person you are becoming may crowd your mind. The new person may not fit in with the old crowd you lived happily with, yet it has not established a new community or soul tribe to live with going forward. At this point, you might feel extremely isolated. If you are not careful, you might get scared, ditch all your efforts, and return to who you were. People love to hang on to familiar pillars and landmarks in their lives, even if they lead to regression. Such behaviour is driven by a sense of isolation. Therefore, recognise it as a delusion and do not fall for it.

There is no going back once you have experienced how it feels to change within you and the accompanying freedom and the benefits. Once you have woken up, you cannot go back to sleep. Once you know something, you cannot undo knowing it. It becomes a new programme, a part of your cellular memory and brain functioning. The NEW YOU would want to feed the hunger for becoming this wonderful new person. The NEW YOU will take control and embrace assurance despite the fears. My advice is to keep improving and growing, one step after another. While on this journey, remember John Bytheway's quote, "Inch by inch life's a cinch, but yard by yard life's hard." Continue becoming your excellent self every day, inch by inch.

MODULE 9: COMPASSION

"There never was any heart truly great and generous that was not also tender and compassionate".

Bishop Robert South

Chapter 13

HUMANITY'S NEED FOR COMPASSION

COMPASSION IS AN intrinsic and necessary emotion needed by humanity and other species. According to verywellmind.com, compassion involves feeling another person's pain and wanting to relieve their suffering[37]. Wikipedia states that "Compassion motivates people to go out of their way to relieve the physical, mental, or emotional pains of others and themselves"[38]. In psychology, compassion is seen as connecting by identifying with another person. Identifying with others can lead to a heightened motivation to relieve their suffering.

A relentless drive for wealth, recognition, and status has led to people becoming more self-centred and concerned with attaining material possessions. Wealth and status are not bad but seeking them at the expense or through the exploitation of others reveals a lack of compassion. Today, many lives are casually taken, showing disrespect for life itself. Young people between the ages of 11 and 16 in urban centres in the UK kill one another for trivial reasons. Mass shootings by young, estranged individuals frequently occur in the USA. It is natural to ask: what happened to our society, and where have we gone wrong? If you ask what we lack in society, the answer is clear: compassion. It seems to have disappeared in society.

Compassion is love full of empathy, understanding, and patience. It drives us to care for one another based on our shared humanity and common needs within a shared universe. Compassion allows us to see that each of us endures difficulties unique to our circumstances but that these difficulties are equally painful. Compassion is about having that intuitive ability to feel others' pain though your issues may be different. It is about recognising that you could be the one facing that challenge and then mustering the will to help the other surmount their problem.

Underlying compassion is the intuitive understanding that the other person's pain is your pain. You must ask yourself whether you understand this because it is personal and real or simply from a theoretical perspective. In other words, compassion is doing unto others what you wish them to do for you. "Do to others as you would have them do to you" is a quote from Jesus in the Bible (Luke 6:31 and Mathew 7:12). Many Christians consider it the Golden Rule of life. Another widely quoted Biblical sentiment is to love your neighbour as you love yourself, which appears in no less than eight portions of the Bible. All these quotes are based on the notion that the self and others are deeply connected. Buddhists have a principle that states that your life and environment while appearing separate to the naked eye, are inseparable[39]. This means that the self and the environment are not two separate entities but one inseparable, united organism, though, on the surface, they appear quite distinct from each other. This unity of self and others becomes the rationale and wellspring for compassion when it is understood.

Compassion, therefore, is an emotion that every human should possess within themselves. We are all capable of showing and expressing compassion. However, our sense of compassion may be eroded due to the philosophies we follow, how we were raised, the prevailing social values, and the experiences we encounter, particularly in early life. Of course, we see people now and again manifesting compassion in the face of natural disasters, even in foreign lands. This proves that we have the capacity for compassion, and all we need is to try to show it as much as possible without the stimulus of an earthquake, flood, or other natural disaster. Compassion is not just a feeling of empathy and wanting to alleviate others' suffering. It does not depend on the recipient of the compassion and the context. We are all capable of doing that, including the worst of us. For example, a murderer can show compassion to his mother, wife, or child. A heartless boss can fail to show compassion to his staff but show it unflinchingly to his family. But the compassionate person does far more. His compassion is not conditional. Becoming truly compassionate requires inner growth.

How Maturity Fosters Compassion

An essential outcome of following the steps in this book is to become consciously compassionate, not just contextually compassionate human beings. After following the steps diligently and practising the skills, you mature into this 'New You' described in the previous chapter. What do I mean by mature? I mean that you become a person who has accepted yourself entirely, everything including your flaws. You have also become self-aware and conscious of your thoughts, behaviours, and emotions. Not only are you aware of your emotions, but you are also aware and sensitive to others' own emotions. By maturing, you come full circle, knowing you are only human. You move away from thinking there is anyone perfect out there or expecting perfection from anyone, least of all you. The self-discovery journey will reveal this to you. When you get to discover and know yourself, you also get to understand others.

Growing, changing, and transforming is not easy, but the benefit is learning a lot about yourself and realising that you are not different from others. In other words, you belong to the human race, and we are all the same in nature and needs, and most of all, we are all connected. You understand that we all experience the same emotions and challenges. Everyone you know or meet is at a particular stage in their growth journey. You discover that as individuals, we all suffer, though differently, due to our personalities and circumstances.

Different forms of growth and development lead to maturity. There is biological growth, which is growing in stature, infant to adult. There is economic growth in wealth and career. There is intellectual growth in thought and wisdom and spiritual growth, which involves growth in your consciousness. I am talking about inner growth akin to spiritual growth, i.e., growth in your thinking, behaviours, wisdom, and the way you use knowledge. When some people grow and prosper economically, become rich, or attain positions of influence in society, they start looking down on others. They sneer at the less fortunate, considering them less worthy, less clever and all-round less important than themselves. Compassion is not a part of the emotional arsenal of such people. Their growth is merely in monetary status and possessions, but they lack inner growth. Unfortunately, that is the growth many aspire to have today.

The growth and maturity I am talking about is the inner maturity that usually manifests as a natural humility and lacks the pomposity of the materially endowed. The awareness from inner growth shows that you are like all other humans and are on earth for a limited period. This is a naturally humbling awareness. Mature people know they are connected to others and the entire universe and shouldn't put themselves or anyone else on a pedestal. This sense of connection becomes a source of great joy and contentment. In short, the mature person who has achieved inner growth becomes what we all desire to be — happy!

The mature individual knows we are all full of flaws and imperfections and are prone to falling and messing up. They know they could be in the other person's place. Maturity teaches you to become non-judgemental, non-condemning, and, most importantly, forgiving. The mature person becomes a patient being who seeks to understand, one who is polite, respectful of life (any life), and down to earth. They want to alleviate other people's suffering in the best way they can from a genuine and deep feeling of compassion. This new being is full of compassion. Like Mother Teresa, who was renowned for her extraordinary compassion, people and leaders of all religions and countries listened when she spoke even on sensitive issues. She was revered all over the world. That is the power of a compassionate being.

The characteristics described so far are a result of inner work and growth. It is rare to find many people who get to this level fully. This level of maturity would be akin to self-actualisation, which is the top level of growth mentioned in Maslow's 'Hierarchy of Needs'. It's like being enlightened.

Why Have We Lost Compassion?

Our world is full of violence. Violence begets violence, anger begets anger, and war escalates to war. There is a common saying that "Hurt people hurt others". On the other hand, compassion can bring love and healing — something our world needs more than anything else. Compassion shown to even the worst people will beget compassion. Note that being compassionate does not mean we condone or excuse the other's behaviour. It means, for example, thinking about the perpetrator of the crime and their circumstances, considering what led to their actions. What kind of people are they? What are their backgrounds, experiences, and so on? We are usually shocked and appalled when we hear a heinous crime has been committed. We are quick to condemn the acts using the harshest words. We typically wish that perpetrators receive the most severe penalty under the law. Most of society feels hatred or disgust for the perpetrators with a 'lock them up and throw away the key' mentality. We usually forget that these people have turned bad for various reasons because no child is born bad. We forget that society itself creates people who behave in monstrous ways. Human beings were originally meant to have compassion towards all living things, but somehow, many people lost this sentiment over time. Sometimes, no compassion is shown, even toward children, the most innocent of society.

As a people, we have trashed the environment we live in and need for our survival in the headlong rush for selfish comforts, convenience, economic growth, and material possessions. We have slowly polluted the environment and are reaping the effects of our excesses. We have lost the innate, most essential component of our being as humans, which is compassion. We have virtually sleep-walked into the loss of this compassion unknowingly and unconsciously. The economic world we live in has slowly caused us to lose this innate feeling of compassion. In pursuit of wealth and fulfilling our needs, parents are not spending time with their children, nor are we modelling good behaviours. Due to the fast-paced life and world we live in, and the day-to-day demands on our lives, children are detached from their parents from a very young age. You find less bonding with the mother, usually the primary caregiver, and little or no breastfeeding. At age 2, the child is put in a nursery, only seeing the parents briefly in the morning and evening. After this, TV, peer groups, and social media engagement take over.

The opportunities for parents to spend quality time with their children have thus greatly reduced as children grow. Add to this the increasing rate of family breakups, domestic violence, and other factors that threaten parental bonding. A lack of attachment from infancy means that children miss that human bond brought by the closeness of another human being, including body warmth. No wonder we have a generation that has lost the human touch. Many young people now fall in love remotely via dating and 'hook-up' apps. Many lack social and communication skills arising from the early experiences of their upbringing. They do not understand love in its essence leading to a lack of compassion.

Maternal support, secure attachment, and harmonious family functioning create an environment where self-compassion can develop. Once self-compassion has developed in a child, there is a far higher possibility of that child exhibiting compassion for others.

I have watched popular CSI investigation programmes and documentaries on serial killers and murder investigations. Interestingly, a common theme runs in most of them. Lack of attachment, early traumatic experience, or childhood abandonment are causative factors for lacking empathy and compassion. The individuals' childhood histories are always coloured by traumatic events or experiences. The stories always show common themes of neglect, domestic abuse, sexual abuse, emotional and physical abuse, and seriously dysfunctional families, some featuring drug and alcohol abuse. Children brought up in such environments with a lack of love, care, and nurturing are more likely to grow into uncompassionate adults. Some of these children are the ones who end up committing hideous crimes because they lacked that essential love, empathy, and care in their childhood. This tells us that how we bring up our young ones will translate into the kind of human beings they become. These qualities of love, care, and compassion are meant to be modelled and learnt early in childhood.

How To Become Compassionate

In a fast-paced and stressful life, we need compassion like never before. Whether you are rich, poor, sick, or in good health, compassion is a universal human requirement. Our world needs it. So, how do we become compassionate human beings? How do we cultivate compassion?

All is not lost because we can grow and cultivate these qualities by re-discovering ourselves, going through the journey of self-discovery, and finding out who we essentially are. This inner questioning will help you re-discover your worth and that of others. You will also discover the shared humanity and the common wisdom (which, sadly, is not common) that we are all passing through this planet, and it is worth leaving a positive impact on it. People who have genuinely discovered themselves become compassionate by how they respond to others or act toward other living things.

However, before you have compassion for others, you have to start with yourself. How? By loving yourself first, forgiving yourself, and being kind to yourself. This is because if you are not compassionate to yourself, you cannot be compassionate to others. In my first chapter on accepting yourself, I talked about discovering your essential worth as a human being, recognising and knowing that you are unique and here for a purpose. We must discover and internalise that we are all equal, regardless of colour, ethnicity, shade, body type, sexual orientation, class, or gender. We must discover and internalise the idea that we can choose to work and heal from our pain, trauma, and painful experiences. We can all choose to do the right things. We must discover that however awful others have been to us, whatever our childhood experiences were, we can choose a different path, a noble path. We can choose love over hate, creation over destruction, life over death, forgiveness over condemnation, patience over haste, understanding over ignorance, and humility over pride and arrogance. We can all choose to do the right thing. We can choose compassion over heartlessness.

I am humbled by the story in the Bible where Jesus was confronted with a woman caught in the act and on the verge of being stoned by the public (mostly men) for adultery. Jesus was quiet at first, and then he wrote a simple sentence in the sand: "Let he who is without sin cast the first stone." The townspeople read the note and walked away, one by one. Jesus then asked the woman, "Has anyone condemned you?" She said, "No one." Then Jesus replied, "Then neither do I. Go and sin no more." This is compassion of the highest order in action.

Here's an example of how a truly compassionate individual views and responds to a mass killing incident. We have had people who have conducted mass shootings of people and children. The media reports usually create mixed emotions, but most people are filled with revulsion and some hatred for the killer, while others are left with pain, anger, bitterness, and resentment. Yet others are dumbfounded and cannot understand why such things happen. Some are unbothered and continue with their lives as if nothing has happened.

A compassionate person naturally abhors the crime, identifies with the pain of the victims, and wants to help alleviate their pain. But they do not stop there. Their response to the perpetrator of the crime is different. No matter how heinous the crime they condemn, they are not so quick to judge the perpetrator. Instead, they are inclined to think about why they committed the crime and ponder further about who the perpetrators are and how they came to conceive and do such a horrific thing. They look at the situation in the round and wonder what can be done to stop further acts of this kind and how the active perpetrator could have been saved from committing this crime. The compassionate mind recognises that we have created these monsters and bear a responsibility to explore what we can do to avoid a repeat of the same. They recognise that there is a human being behind the crime and that something must have gone very wrong for the person to do what they did. They are not quick to condemn or judge the person. This type of response requires total compassion that can only come from having done the inner work.

The overall acceptance concept and the steps derived from it, which you have been reading in this book, are geared to bring you to this point. One of the desired outcomes of going through this journey is for you to become a conscious and compassionate human being. At this level, you experience love for humanity, identify yourself with others, and actively want to help others. When filled with compassion, you start giving and contributing to society. You want to do good and make a difference in people's lives. You want to touch lives in the best way you can.

Please note that at this stage, you will feel moved by world problems and various injustices in the world. You may feel like solving all the world's problems. But realise that you cannot solve the world's systemic issues alone. Nevertheless, you can make a difference starting from where you are by doing what you can and what you are being called to do. You start impacting your world starting from your circle of influence. It does not matter how small or big that circle is, whether it is your family, village, constituency, district, country, or continent. When you start from where you are, you can make ripples. Have you ever thrown a pebble into a pond? No matter how small the pebble was, it caused ripples in the water. That is what will happen when you show compassion and make a difference in people's lives starting from where you are.

No matter how small, even if it's one person, it will make ripples. By showing compassion to one child, you never know who or what that kid or person will become. You can divert a disaster by showing compassion to one person. Many stories are told of people planning to do horrible things, but they changed their minds when shown human compassion. Impact your world by showing compassion wherever you are, whenever you can, and whichever way you can. A journey of a thousand miles starts with the first step.

Overall, compassion is great for both the giver and the receiver. I feel good whenever I give or help freely from the heart. When you also get a thank you from the receiver, it adds to the good feeling. I would like to believe it is the same for everybody. You feel happier when you give, volunteer, support, advise, or show compassion to another. Buddhists say when you light a lantern for the other, you also light your way. A boss who is compassionate to his employees creates a good working environment. Contributing to a good cause is a show of compassion that improves your psychological wellbeing. Likewise, the receiver feels good and supported during their difficult times.

Compassion, therefore, is powerful. It brings a contribution that leads to connection, love, oneness, and harmony in a society. I sincerely hope the steps in this book set you on a path to becoming a compassionate being.

MODULE 10: EVOLVE

"The whole point of being alive is to evolve into the complete person you were intended to be."

Oprah Winfrey

Chapter 14

THE EVOLVED BEING

EVOLVING IS A natural process, and according to Merriam-Webster's dictionary, it is to progress, grow, emerge, mature, blossom, and unfold or develop[40]. Charles Darwin's book on the human species theorised that humans evolved from apes to upright men to men with ability and later men with intelligence. The current genus of man is the 'homo sapiens' or 'man with intelligence or the capacity for thought'. Darwin is hugely respected for his contributions to ideas on the evolution of man. However, some critique the theory by suggesting there was a missing link in evolution when man evolved from his apelike ancestor to become the creature we are today. Nevertheless, his theory perfectly illustrates evolution as a process of gradual growth over time.

In his great work, 'The Evolution of Species', it is interesting to note that Darwin talked of a process of natural selection. By this, he meant that by the process of the survival of the fittest, only those species that evolved most efficiently to meet the challenges posed by their environments were selected to survive and thrive. Natural selection implies that those who did not evolve became destined for extinction over time. So again, we see the natural imperative for man and other species to prioritise their evolution. It is a vital survival mechanism. Those who evolve, survive and grow but those who don't, fall by the wayside.

Undoubtedly, we have advanced as a species over time, simply by reference to the world we have created, the technology we now employ, and the cultural leaps of thought and lifestyle over the space of 2 decades, let alone one century. If people from 300 years ago woke up in our world today, they wouldn't recognise the world we now live in. Evolving is a process of gradual development. We develop as a people in every generation and as individuals in our unique way. Some people consciously develop and grow themselves, while others are forced to by nature or life circumstances. It must also be said that some people don't develop at all.

The evolution I discuss in this book is the kind you consciously choose to bring about. Following the steps outlined in this book, you gradually become an evolved person by your own will and choice. You move from being good to being better to being your best. You become, through this evolution, the best version of yourself or what you call an actualised human being. The renowned behaviourist Abraham Maslow called this self-transcendence – a situation in which you consciously choose to develop yourself, putting in the work to create value in your life and positively impact the world around you. As I said earlier in the book, your world could be your family, village, company, society and nation. It all depends on what your horizons are and your ambitions.

Our world is large and diverse, but its crucial changes are driven by less than 10% of self-conscious people who are often called Great Leaders. These are people who have boldly walked the journey of self-discovery. They know who they are, why they are here, and the divine potential they carry. They have matured and transcended themselves and consciously chosen to leave great footprints. They have evolved as human beings. They have dared to ask themselves deep and difficult questions and have not been afraid to face the truth or the challenges that come with the answers. They have not shied away from taking on the world and its systemic complications but have shown up and produced astounding results through their efforts. Now we call them 'great' due to what they have done. They have impacted our world and made it a better place for us.

Evolving requires that we treat personal development as a life goal. It is the day-to-day application of self-awareness and self-control, showing behaviours that express 'good character' which follow moral values. It is sharing your skills and knowledge, offering your gifts and talents to others, and making a difference in other people's lives. It is showing generosity, compassion, integrity and fairness to others. It promotes and encourages others. These are all acts of self-transcendence.

Evolving is taking actions that exceed other people's expectations. It is moving from mediocrity and making a conscious decision to put your heart and soul into everything you do, making it a habit to let your work reflect the high standards you hold for yourself. Finally, evolving means moving from a mentality of service to self alone to one of service to self and others.

When you evolve, you gravitate towards the ever-changing world and its needs, re-thinking solutions and becoming creative and innovative. It is being flexible, adaptive and moving with the times. You learn new ways and methods to be of service to humanity. Evolving requires that you continuously re-evaluate where you are vis-a-vis where you are going and who you want to become. Every day becomes a learning experience. Evolving is a never-ending, continuous process.

Ten Characteristics of An Evolving Person

1. They strive to have a life worth living. They aspire to have a well-lived life.
2. They have value-based goals.
3. They are full of gratitude.
4. They have great self-control and are in charge of their emotions.
5. They have a mission to accomplish their life vision.
6. Failure does not hinder them. Rather, they see failure as a growth process.
7. They stop to reflect and can re-evaluate.
8. They are humble with their gifts and therefore share their gifts and passions with others.
9. They take time to pray and meditate.
10. They endeavour to bring out the best in others.

Are you evolving? Keep on evolving.

CONCLUSION

"Run to brilliance. Sprint to excellence. Soar to transcendence."

Matshona Dhliwayo

I F YOU HAVE come this far, you have gotten the gist of this book. This book is about your personal growth using the ACCEPTANCE programme. The program was born out of severe pain, loss and bereavement. It brings together my personal and professional experiences. I was an ordinary mother and therapist going through a tough time and despair. With a surviving son to care for, I was forced to rise and live again to fulfil my responsibilities to him and myself. I had to accept the reality of my life and decide how to move forward at a time when I felt emotionally and spiritually paralysed. I first had to accept my eldest son's terminal illness, which led to his departure from this world. I then had to admit that I was not dealing with it very well. If I were not careful, I would sacrifice everything, including my younger son, who still needed me.

My arrival at that place of acceptance and using the methods outlined in this book helped me move forward from a state of abject paralysis. It enabled me to think differently, change my mindset, and change my life. I stepped out of the deadlock and became a different, more evolved person. My inner transformation arose from following the steps described in the ten modules in this book.

I became stronger, better grounded, and more confident in myself. Life started to have meaning, and I felt joy again. When I realised what I was experiencing, I sat down and figured out what was happening to me. It became clear that the change I was experiencing resulted from two things. First, I had accepted and acknowledged my reality. Secondly, I had a burning desire for change in my life, and I applied the skills I developed at work to my everyday life. As a result, those skills took on greater meaning and weight in my circumstances. If acceptance of my reality combined with a desire to change my life by applying proven methods could change an ordinary mum like me, it could also help others who find themselves paralysed by their circumstances. It dawned on me that anyone at a total loss or crossroads could also find a breakthrough.

I have used the lessons distilled in this book to coach my clients (1:1 and group) on the A.C.C.E.P.T.A.N.C.E programme. It is a step-by-step self-discovery and personal development process that is easy to follow. I start by coaching you to **accept** yourself fully and to become authentic. I help you discover and live by your **core values**. Next is building and developing your **character** or personal brand, managing your **emotions**, identifying and changing your perceptions, and mastering your **thoughts.** We dive deep into these modules enabling you to find and apply the skills specifically required for your unique situation. The other part of the programme covers how to take **action** to become the **New You.** This leads to the birth of a **compassionate** human being that is authentically the real you. Finally, the programme addresses **evolving** and blossoming into the transformed, value-creating You. The ACCEPTANCE process transforms you into the excellent self you can be.

Nobody is exempt from life's challenges, and we all need these steps to navigate the deadlocks we encounter. The ACCEPTANCE programme will help you transcend these challenges, bring out the full potential inside of you, build resilience and live a happy, purposeful, and fulfilling life. The programme is geared toward bringing out the tough person in you. Like Robert Schuller[41] said, "Tough times never last, but tough people do."

I sincerely hope you find this book helpful. For practical 1:1 or group coaching on the ACCEPTANCE programme and how to leverage its lasting benefits, please contact me at www.veronicakararwa.com. I promise you will not regret it.

BIBLIOGRAPHIC RESOURCES

Below are the references made to authors, personalities and sources of information made in this book. This is not an exhaustive bibliography but may assist those who wish to engage in further reading related to the ACCEPTANCE Programme.

INTRODUCTION

1. Baranski, T. (2023) What is life? Philosophy Now Magazine. Available at: https://philosophynow. org/issues/101/What_Is_Life#:~:text=Life%20 is%20the%20aspect%20of,for%20physical%20 and%20conscious%20development

2. Wikipedia is a free online encyclopaedia compiled by volunteers. It Is frequently used throughout the book to render simple, popularly given definitions of words, events and phrases. This is done to provide definitions and explanations with the widest possible appeal and to which people can relate. https://en.wikipedia.org/wiki/ Meaning_of_life.

3. **Dr Paul T. Wong** is a Canadian registered psychologist who originated Meaning-Centred Counselling and Therapy (MCCT), an integrative, existential, and positive approach to counselling, coaching, and psychotherapy. Dr Paul is also the Founding President of the International Network on Personal Meaning (INPM) and the International Society for Existential Psychology and Psychotherapy (ISEPP).

4. **Dr Ravi Zacharias** March 26, 1946 – May 19, 2020) was born in India and immigrated to Canada with his family twenty years later. Well-versed in comparative religions, cults, and philosophy, he was chair of Evangelism and Contemporary Thought at Alliance Theological Seminary for three and a half years. Dr Zacharias has been honoured by conferring a Doctor of Divinity degree both from Houghton College, NY, and from Tyndale College and Seminary, Toronto, and a Doctor of Laws degree from Asbury College in Kentucky.

5. **The Holy Bible,** NEW INTERNATIONAL VERSION®, NIV® Copyright © 1973, 1978, 1984, 2011 by Biblica, Inc.® Used by permission. All rights reserved worldwide.

    "I praise you because I am fearfully and wonderfully made; your works are wonderful, I know that full well." Psalm 139:14

    "Before I formed you in the womb I knew you, before you were born I set you apart; I appointed you as a prophet to the nations." Jeremiah 1:5

CHAPTER 1: FACING MY CROSSROADS

6. **Afro Caribbean Leukaemia Trust (ACLT):** Cofounded by Beverley De-Gayle OBE and Orin Lewis OBE in 1996. ACLT is a 40-plus times award-winning charity committed to providing hope to patients living with blood cancer and illnesses where a matched donor (stem cell, blood or organ) is required to save a life. Their work is driven by a belief that no one should die waiting for a donor to become available. https://aclt.org/

CHAPTER 2: WHAT IS ACCEPTANCE?

7. **Elisabeth Kübler-Ross** (July 8, 1926 – August 24, 2004) was a Swiss-American psychiatrist, a pioneer in near-death studies, and author of the internationally best-selling book, On Death and Dying (1969), where she first discussed her theory of the five stages of grief, also known as the "Kübler-Ross model". https://en.wikipedia. org/wiki/Elisabeth_K%C3%BCbler-Ross https://www.ekrfoundation. org/5-stages-of-grief/5-stages-grief/

8. **Abraham Maslow and the Hierarchy of Needs:** Abraham Maslow was a behavioural Scientist who suggested in 1943 that human motivation could be explained as a hierarchy of needs in which higher needs like love, belonging, esteem and self-actualisation would not be pursued until lower needs like physiological, bodily, safety and security needs were met. Maslow, A. H. (1943). A theory of human motivation. Psychological Review, 50, 370–396. Maslow, A. H. (1969). The farther reaches of human nature. Journal of Transpersonal Psychology,1(1), 1–9.

9. **McLeod, S. (2023).** Maslow's Hierarchy Of Needs. Available at: https://www.simplypsychology.org/maslow.html

10. **Cherry, K (2023).**
11 Characteristics of Self-Actualized People. Available at: https://www.verywellmind.com/characteristics-of-self-actualized-people-2795963

CHAPTER 3: THE FIRST W OF SELF-ACCEPTANCE

11. **Rosa Louise McCauley Parks** (February 4, 1913 – October 24, 2005) was an American activist in the civil rights movement best known for her pivotal role in the Montgomery bus boycott. Parks became an NAACP activist in 1943, participating in several high-profile civil rights campaigns. On December 1, 1955, in Montgomery, Alabama, Parks rejected bus driver James F. Blake's order to vacate a row of four seats in the "coloured" section in favour of a White passenger once the "White" section was filled. https://en.wikipedia.org/wiki/Rosa_Parks

12. **Nicholas James Vujicic**   Nicholas James Vujicic is an Australian Christian evangelist and motivational and keynote speaker born with tetra-amelia syndrome, a rare disorder characterized by the absence of arms and legs. Nick persevered through life's challenges and discovered key principles which enabled him to find his purpose and turn obstacles into opportunities, making him one of the most sought-after keynote speakers in the world. https://nickvujicic.com/

CHAPTER 4: SELF-ACCEPTANCE
– OTHER FOUR 'W's

13. **Wayne Walter Dyer** (May 10, 1940 – August 29, 2015) was an American self-help author and motivational speaker. Dyer completed an Ed.D. in guidance and counselling at Wayne State University in 1970. Early in his career, he worked as a high school guidance counsellor and went on to run a successful private therapy practice. His first book, *Your Erroneous Zones* (1976), is one of the best-selling books

of all time, with an estimated 100 million copies sold. In addition, he published 20 other best-selling books.

14. **Deepak Chopra MD, MD, FACP, FRCP** founded The Chopra Foundation, a non-profit entity for research on well-being and humanitarianism, and Chopra Global, a modern-day health company at the intersection of science and spirituality, is a world-renowned pioneer in integrative medicine and personal transformation.

15. **Myles Munroe, OBE** (20 April 1954 – 9 November 2014). He was a Bahamian evangelist and ordained minister, avid professor of the Kingdom of God, author, speaker and leadership consultant. He founded and led the Bahamas Faith Ministries International (BFMI) and Myles Munroe International (MMI).

16. **Genesis 1:26-28 (NIV):** Then God said, "Let us make mankind in our image, in our likeness, so that they may rule over the fish in the sea and the birds in the sky, over the livestock and all the wild animals, and over all the creatures that move along the ground." So God created mankind in

his own image, in the image of God he created them; male and female he created them. God blessed them and said to them, "Be fruitful and increase in number; fill the earth and subdue it. Rule over the fish in the sea and the birds in the sky and over every living creature that moves on the ground."

17. **John 1: 12 (NIV):** "Yet to all who did receive him, to those who believed in his name, he gave the right to become children of God—."

18. **Proverbs 29:18 (KJV).** "Where there is no vision, the people perish: but he that keepeth the law, happy is he."

19. **Ecclesiastes 10:19 (NIV).** "A feast is made for laughter, wine makes life merry, and money is the answer for everything."

20. **Jim Rohn** - Emanuel James Rohn (September 17, 1930 – December 5, 2009), professionally known as Jim Rohn, was an American entrepreneur, author and motivational speaker. See: https://en.wikipedia.org/wiki/Jim_Rohn

CHAPTER 5: WHAT ARE YOUR CORE VALUES?

21. See Genesis 37 and 39-45

CHAPTER 6: THE VALUE OF CHARACTER

22. **Ralph Waldo Emerson** was an American Transcendentalist poet, philosopher and essayist during the 19th century. One of his best-known essays is "Self-Reliance."

CHAPTER 7: MASTER YOUR EMOTIONS

23. **Marsha Linehan** (born May 5, 1943) is an American psychologist and author. She is the creator of dialectical behaviour therapy (DBT), a type of psychotherapy that combines cognitive restructuring with acceptance, mindfulness, and shaping.

24. **Daniel Goleman** is an internationally known psychologist who frequently lectures to professional groups, business audiences, and on college campuses. His 1995 book, Emotional Intelligence, was on The New York Times bestseller list for a year and a half, with over 5,000,000 copies in print worldwide in 40 languages and has

been a best seller in many countries. Goleman has also written books on self-deception, creativity, transparency, meditation, social and emotional learning, ecoliteracy and the ecological crisis. https://www.danielgoleman.info/biography/

25. **Gabor Mate - Gabor Maté CM** (born January 6, 1944) is a Canadian physician and author. He has a background in family practice and a special interest in childhood development, trauma and potential lifelong impacts on physical and mental health, including autoimmune disease, cancer, and attention deficit hyperactivity.

CHAPTER 9: YOUR THOUGHTS ARE POWERFUL

26. **Proverbs 23:7 (KJV):** "For as he thinketh in his heart, so is he: Eat and drink, saith he to thee; but his heart is not with thee."

27. **James Allen** (28 November 1864 – 24 January 1912) was a British philosophical writer known for his inspirational books and poetry and as a pioneer of the self-help movement. His best-known work, As a Man Thinketh, has been mass-produced since its publication in 1902. It has been a source of

inspiration to motivational and self-help authors.

28. https://en.wikipedia.org/wiki/Thought
Thomas Newcomen
https://www.bbc.co.uk/history/historic_figures/
newcomen_thomas.shtml

30. **Oliver Napoleon Hill** (October 26, 1883 – November 8, 1970) was an American self-help author. He is best known for his book Think and Grow Rich (1937), among the best-selling self-help books ever. Hill's works insisted that fervid expectations are essential to improving one's life. Most of his books were promoted as expounding principles to achieve "success".

CHAPTER 11: WINNING WHERE OTHERS HAVE FAILED

31. **Melanie Robbins** (née Schneeberger on October 6, 1968) is an American podcast host, author, motivational speaker, and former lawyer. She is known for her TEDx talk, "How to Stop Screwing Yourself Over", and her books, The 5 Second Rule and The High 5 Habit, and host of The Mel Robbins Podcast. https://en.wikipedia.org/wiki/Mel_Robbins

CHAPTER 12: HAPPY NEW YOU!

32. **Kevin Kararwa Leukaemia Trust** (KKLT) was established in 2015. It seeks to engage with BME (black & minority ethnic communities) to raise awareness of Leukaemia, educate about bone marrow/stem cell donation, and encourage individuals to join the stem cell registry. The aim is to increase the BME community's blood cancer survival rate. https://www.kkltrust.org/

33. Richard Duane Warren (born January 28, 1954) is an American Southern Baptist Evangelical Christian pastor and author. He is the founder of Saddleback Church, an evangelical Baptist m egachurch in Lake Forest, California.

34. Stephen Richards Covey (October 24, 1932 – July 16, 2012) was an American educator, author, businessman, and speaker. His most popular book is 'The 7 Habits of Highly Effective People'.

35. Pauline Joyce Meyer (née Hutchison; June 4, 1943) is an American Charismatic Christian author, speaker, and president of Joyce Meyer Ministries. Joyce and her husband, Dave, have four grown children and live outside St. Louis, Missouri.

Her ministry is headquartered near the St. Louis suburb of Fenton, Missouri.

36. Thomas Dexter Jakes (born June 9, 1957), known as T. D. Jakes, is an American non-denominational Christian preacher. He is the Senior Pastor of The Potter's House, a non-denominational American megachurch.

CHAPTER 13: HUMANITY'S NEED FOR COMPASSION

37. Kerry C. (2021). What is Compassion? Available at https://www.verywellmind.com/what-is-compassion-5207366
38. https://en.wikipedia.org/wiki/Compassion
39. The Buddhist principle of the oneness of life and its environment was taken from the SGI Buddhist Dictionary.

CHAPTER 14: THE EVOLVED BEING

40. https://www.merriam-webster.com/dictionary/evolution

CONCLUSION

41. **Robert Harold Schuller** (September 16, 1926 - April 2, 2015) was an American Christian televangelist, pastor, motivational speaker, and author. In his five decades of television, Schuller was principally known for the weekly Hour of Power television program, which he began hosting in 1970 until his retirement in 2010.